CAMRA'S

BEER

Anthology

Edited by Roger Protz

CAMRA
BOOKS

Published by the Campaign for Real Ale Ltd.
230 Hatfield Road
St Albans
Hertfordshire AL1 4LW

www.camra.org.uk/books

ISBN 978-1-85249-333-2

A CIP catalogue record for this book is available from the British Library

Printed and bound in Poland by Latitude Press Ltd

Picture credits: Alexander_P/Shutterstock: p12, 47, 59, 76, 82, 85, 101, 112;
AVA Bitter/Shutterstock: p122

Head of Publishing: Simon Hall
Project Editor: Katie Button
Editorial Assistance: Susannah Lord, Julie Hudson
Design: Linda Storey, Top Floor Design Ltd
Copyright Consultant: Naomi Korn, Copyright Consultancy Ltd
Sales & Marketing: David Birkett

Contents

Introduction

> Strike thy bosom, sage! and tell,
> What is bliss, and which the way?...
> When the hoary Sage reply'd,
> 'Come, my lad, and drink some beer.'
>
> **Samuel Johnson, 1777**

This is a celebration of the world's oldest and most popular alcoholic drink and of the places – pubs, bars, inns and taverns – where it can best be enjoyed. Beer is not just rooted in history, it has helped frame civilisation. It was the need to grown grain in order to make life's staples – beer and bread – that encouraged nomadic people at the dawn of time to settle down and establish communities to grow early types of barley and wheat. And as soon as beer was brewed in the Old World, people wrote about it, composed hymns and songs in its praise, and created gods and goddesses to protect it.

In the centuries that followed, as brewing spread to Europe, Celts, Picts, Jutes, Saxons and Angles not only drank copious amounts of ale but celebrated it in rhyme and song. The Romans in Britain established one of the earliest forms of communal drinking place, the taberna or tavern, where beer as well as wine was consumed. From pre-Roman Britain, through the Germanic and Norse invasions, and the arrival of the Normans, ale and beer have been drunk and recorded. William the Conqueror's *Domesday Book*, a survey of the life, habits and working practises of the inhabitants of England, records a vast army of small brewers in towns and cities, hovels and manor houses.

Many handed down their recipes while consumers recorded their praise or dislike of the end product. Clearly, CAMRA and its *Good Beer Guide* have doughty forebears!

From such early work as the *Tunnyng of Elynour Rummyng* and *Gammer Gurton's Needle*, through the *Canterbury Tales* and on to Shakespeare's plays with their many references to good ale, it is clear that making and drinking beer had become deeply embedded in British society. And as Mistress Quickly's Boar's Head in *Henry IV* shows, inns and taverns occupied a central role in the pageant of daily life.

The development of the market economy, beginning in Tudor times, intensifying under Cromwell and finding full flower in the 18th and 19th centuries, saw Britain become one of the principle brewing nations of the world, a role widely celebrated in verse as well as prose. Neighbouring Ireland added its own distinctive beer styles and voices, with the likes of James Joyce and Flann O'Brien in the 20th century describing the joys of stout and 'a pint of plain'.

The development of porter in the 18th century and pale ale 100 years later, along with coaching inns, gin palaces and the modern pub, have all encouraged writing that is both eloquent and at times riotously amusing, especially in the hands of Charles Dickens. He devoted a vast amount of time to recording the activities of drinkers and innkeepers: his dedication to the cause is an inspiration to all aspiring writers on the subject.

In more recent times, George Orwell and Dylan Thomas, among others, have described the pleasures of beer and pubs while the turn of the 21st century has seen a bevy – *le mot juste!* – of young writers adding fresh voices to the cause.

With a veritable explosion of beer styles and passionate craft brewers throughout the world, there has never been greater interest in the subject. There is just cause to eulogise a drink rich in history and literature. Raise a glass and join the celebration.

Roger Protz
St Albans, April 2016

A HISTORY
OF BEER

I feel wonderful, drinking beer
In a blissful mood
With joy in my heart
And a happy liver

These words, written by a Sumerian poet circa 3000BC, show that beer was an integral part of daily life in the Old World of North Africa and the Middle East. A great deal is known about brewing in such countries as ancient Egypt, Babylonia and Mesopotamia as a result of translations of tablets with cuneiform writing. From these translations we learn that, in that vast region, hunter-gatherers settled into communities to grow grain with the specific aim of making bread and beer. Brewing is therefore as old as civilisation and helped to keep people healthy at a time when water was insanitary. Female gods, such as the Goddess Ninkasi in Babylonia, protected beer while brewers, who were mainly women, were given a special hieroglyph 𓏏𓊪 (fty).

As brewing progressed, the methods used underwent important changes. While hops were not used, brewers balanced the sweetness of grain with plants and spices. In 'On Beer and Brewing Techniques in Ancient Mesopotamia', written by Hartmann and Oppenheim in 1950, the authors' research shows that brewers had learnt to turn barley into malt, which enabled much improved beer to be made. They added that the 'preparation of malt won from barley is the all-important process in the Mesopotamian brewery of the *second and third millennia. Malting belongs to an important technological stage in the development of methods for the preparation of vegetable foodstuff.'*

The importance of written evidence about brewing in the Old World was emphasised by the American anthropologist and beer writer Alan D Eames, author of The Secret Life of Beer, *published in 1995. Eames toured caves in Egypt and helped translate ancient tablets. As a result of his studies, he wrote: 'Protected by alcohol, beer had a palatability lasting far longer than any other foodstuff. A vitamin-rich porridge, daily beer drinking increased both health and longevity, reducing disease and malnutrition... It was this appetite for beer-making material that led to crop cultivation, settlement and agriculture. Ten thousand years ago, for example, barley was domesticated and worshipped as a god in the highlands of the southern Levant. Thus was beer the driving force that led nomadic people into village life. With the creation of writing – stylus on wet clay tablet – beer, its history and mystery, became a large part of ancient man's literary repertoire.'*

We found a wonderful small bakery willing to rent to us. We moved our team in and we made 5,000 little bappir loaves from recipes as best we could define it, as if we were brewing in 3000BC. In this bread there is raw barley flour, for barley was overwhelmingly the grain of the ancient world. There's a little bit of roasted barley because the husk on the barley is difficult to get off and we know from the ancient Sumerian records that roasted barley was common. We used a little bit of malted barley because we knew they had malted barley and we had to make the fundamental decision that our bread should use the kind of things we knew they had and, most important, the bread should taste good.

But barley cannot be baked into bread with a dry centre unless you make almost paper-thin pancake. We asked the experts and we suddenly figured out that this type of bread is twice baked. The Italian word for biscuit, biscotto, means 'twice baked'. We made a big thick pie in the oven in the bakery. We made about 1,000 of these. We let them cool and cut them into strips and about an hour later we baked them again. By the end of the day we had a little over 5,000 of these little loaves. A few days later we put them into the mash tun in our brewery along with some malted barley, which you need for the enzymes to make the sugar, and we made a beer with no hops because we knew from the experts that there were no hops in Sumeria.

The fact there were no hops made us a little nervous but we knew they had dates and we knew from a song from ancient Sumeria, that was one of our key sources, that they used a sweet material. The song is a hymn to the Goddess of Brewing. Her name was Ninkasi. So using this hymn to Ninkasi, which dated from 1800BC, we saw that she added sweetness twice to the beer. We knew the Sumerians had honey and had dates. So we put honey in the bread and then we put dates in the beer because we thought that might gives the beer a little flavour – not quite like hops, but a spicy flavour.

It wasn't a wonderful beer but it was an interesting beer and one of its more interesting qualities was a slightly aromatic bouquet of dates. We put all this bappir bread in the mash tun and we started cooking it and I can tell it was a very eerie feeling, as though we were rubbing the magic lamp. We were calling up the ancient words of brewing. We had called up the Goddess of Beer, Ninkasi, and we did it with a sense of respect for recreating the ancient art of brewing.

Fritz Maytag quoted in *The Ale Trail*, Roger Protz, 1995

In the 1990s, Fritz Maytag, owner of the Anchor Brewery in San Francisco and widely regarded as the main instigator of the American beer revolution, brewed a beer based on an ancient Sumerian recipe found on a clay tablet.

So, if people didn't settle down to take up farming, why then did they embark on this entirely new way of living? We have no idea – or actually, we have lots of ideas, but we don't know if any of them are right. According to Felipe Fernández-Armesto, at least thirty-eight theories have been put forward to explain why people took to living in communities: that they were driven to it by climatic change, or by a wish to stay near their dead, or by a powerful desire to brew and drink beer, which could only be indulged by staying in one place.

At Home: A Short History of Private Life, **Bill Bryson, 2010**

After water and tea, beer is the third most popular drink in the world. This should not be surprising, as beer is also the most complex and varied of drinks. It can taste like lemons or smoke, coffee or coconuts, bananas or bread, chilies or ginger. Beer can be crisply acidic and earthy, or it can be bracingly bitter and spectacularly aromatic. It can evince a mere pickle of carbonation or flourish on the palate into a fine mousse. It can be enjoyed days after it was brewed or emerge from a bottle more than a century later and produce rapturous delight.

Wine, beer's great rival and table companion, despite its many wonders, cannot begin to approach beer's variety of flavor, aroma, and texture. Because beer can taste like almost anything, it brings superior talents to the dining table. Beer does not resemble wine so much as it resembles music. Beer predates human civilisation and may well have had a hand in creating it. Beer was primary in the minds of ancient peoples, who carved word of it into stone, painted images of it upon temple walls, built cities fuelled by its manufacture, and carried it with them into the afterlife. Beer built castles in Bavaria, great ships upon the Baltic Sea, the power of the Hanseatic League, and modern industry in London. Many of the American founding fathers brewed beer, and it has graced the tables of the White House for more than 200 years. Across the sweep of world history, at the cutting edge of technology, on the tables of the rich and the poor, in almost every human situation of any real note, you will find beer.

Oxford Companion to Beer, **Garrett Oliver, 2012**

Garrett Oliver is the brewmaster at the Brooklyn Brewery in New York City and the author of The Brewmaster's Table.

Ac Beton the Brewestere bad him good morwe
And axed of hym with that, whiderward he wode.
'To holi cherche,' quod he, 'for to here masse,
And sithern I wole be shryven and synne namore.'
'I have gode ale, gossib,' quod she, 'Glotoun, wiltow assaye?'
'Hastow aughte in thi purs any hote spices?'
'I have peper and pionés,' quod she, 'and a pounde of garlike,
A ferthyngworth of fennelseed for fastyngdayes.'

Piers Plowman, William Langland, c.1370–90

In the Middle Ages, ale was brewed with spices such as pepper, garlic and fennel. In Piers Plowman *Glowton [Glutton] is accosted on his way to church by Breton the Brewster who invites him in to her tavern for 'good ale and gossip'.*

> A knight of Cailes, a gentleman of Wales,
> And a laird of the north countree,
> A yeoman of Kent with his yearly rent
> Will buy them out all three.

Hops started to replace other flavourings in beer when it was found that the hop plant, as well delivering delightful aromas and flavours to beer, also contained resins and tannins that helped keep beer free from infection. Dutch traders brought hop plants to south-east England and the first hop gardens were laid out in Kent in 1520. Hop growing became a profitable business, as a rhyme of the time suggests.

Whereas you cannot make above 8-9 gallons of indifferent ale from 1 bushel of malt, you may draw 18-20 gallons of very good beer... If your ale may endure a fortnight, your beer through the benefit of the hop, shall continue a month, and what grace it yieldeth to the taste, all men may judge that have sense in their mouths. And if controversy be betwixt Beer and Ale, which of them shall have the place of pre-eminence, it sufficeth for the glory and commendation of Beer that, here in our own country, ale giveth place unto it and that most part of our countrymen do abhor and abandon ale as a loathsome drink.

The Perfite Platforme of a Hoppe Garden, Reynold Scot, 1574

It was the profitability of hopped beer that led to the decline of ale, which was flavoured with herbs and spices. The better keeping qualities of hopped beer meant less malt was used, an important cost consideration.

Ale is made of malt and water and they which do put any other things to ale than is rehearsed except yeast, barm or godisgood, doth sophistical their ale. Ale for an Englishman is a natural drink. Ale must have these properties: it must be fresh and clear; it must not be ropey or smokey nor must it have no weft nor tail. Ale should not be drunk under five days old; new ale is unwholesome for all men and sour ale and dead ale that which doth stand the tilt is good for no man. Barley malt maketh better ale than oaten malt or any other corn duff. It doth engender gross humours but yet it maketh a man strong.

Beer is made of malt, of hops and water. It is the natural drink for a Dutche man. And now of late days it is much used in England to the detriment of many English people. Specially it killeth them which be troubled with colic and a stone and a strangulion for the drink is a cold drink yet it doth make a man fat and doth inflate the bellye as it doth appear by the Dutchman's faces and bellyes. If the beer is well served and be fined, and not new it doth qualify heat of the liver.

A Dyetary of Health, Andrew Boord, 1542

Unhopped ale nevertheless had its supporters, as this 16th century book confirms. 'Barm' and 'godisgood' are both ancient names for yeast. 'Dutche' or 'Dutch', meant Germans, not people from the Netherlands.

A simple visit to a four-generation old hop farm outside Poperinge can be as good a reminder as any that brewing in Belgium is changing. 'Ten years ago, the breweries here brewed mostly pils beer,' says hop farmer Benedikte Coutigny who runs the Hoppecruyt farm in the village of Proven with her husband,

Wout Desmyter. 'But since then they have been brewing more special beers and they need other types of hops.'

A decade ago, Benedikte and Wout relied on a distributor of their hops for information on the varieties in demand. 'There was a shift in focus from the brewers to aroma hops', says Benedikte. 'But all the farmers were growing bitterness hops, so the price was very bad.'

Since they started working directly with the breweries, all that has changed. Where once the entire farm was dominated by bitterness hops, now they constitute only one of the farm's 7.5 hectares. The rest are aroma hops. 'We grow 12 different varieties now,' says Benedikte. 'At the moment we're busy with Centennial. Chinook is also in demand. Wout is out in the fields now cutting the first shoots of Challenger.'

Their farming portfolio has been extended to cattle and brussels sprouts but perhaps their most interesting diversification in the last few years has been the cultivation of hop shoots, the white shoots of the hop plant now considered a regional culinary specialty. Freshly picked for us by Benedikte, they taste fresh and earthy, not unlike a white bean sprout. 'They are best fried', Benedikte says. 'But with no oil, so that they are dry and crispy.'

'From Bitter to Aromatic', **Brendán Kearney**,
Belgian Beer & Food, 2016

Hops have become a key ingredient in beer, and hop gardens an essential part of the rural economy. But brewing trends change over time and hop farmers have had to adapt, as reported by award-winning beer blogger Brendán Kearney. Brendán is from Northern Ireland but is now resident in Ghent, Belgium, where he writes the blog Belgian Smaak (Belgian Taste) with his partner Elisa Depypere. In 2015 he was named Beer Writer of the Year by the British Guild of Beer Writers.

THE PEOPLE'S BEVERAGE

Beer is deeply ingrained in the culture and history of the British Isles. Whether it was consumed in the home or a tavern, people talked about ale and beer, and wrote copiously about it. It was the people's drink: imported wine was far too expensive for the majority of the populace but ale – at a time when water and milk were unfit to drink – made with ingredients plucked from the surrounding fields, refreshed and kept people healthy.

From the earliest times, the pleasures of ale and beer have been recorded for posterity. Chaucer, Shakespeare, Dickens and Housman are just a few of the literary luminaries that have voiced their views on the delights of a tankard containing the juices of the barley and the hop. They are joined today by a small army of writers with a different aim: they are not commenting on beer in passing, as part of a wider literary endeavour, but are dedicated full time to evaluating, researching, analysing, promoting and championing beer.

Caesar affirms that all other Nations of the known World drink Wine or Water only; but the Britains, saith he, (who yet have Vines enough) make no other use of them, but for Arbours in their Gardens, or to adorn and set forth their houses, drinking a high and mighty liquor, different from that of any other Nation, made of Barley and Water, which being not so subtle in its operations as Wine, yet did warm as much, and nourish more, leaving space enough for the performance of many great Actions, before it quite vanquisht the Spirits.

Divi Britannici, **Sir Winston Churchill, 1675**

Julius Caesar was complementary of British beer, as recounted in 1675 by Sir Winston Churchill, father of the Duke of Marlborough and an ancestor of the wartime Prime Minister.

Life isn't all beer and skittles; but beer and skittles, or something better of the same sort, must form a good part of every Englishman's education.

Tom Brown's Schooldays, **Thomas Hughes, 1859**

O GUDE ale comes and gude ale goes,
Gude ale gars me sell my hose,
Sell my hose, and pawn my shoon,
Gude ale keeps my heart aboon.
I had sax owsen in a pleugh,
And they drew a' weel enough;
I sell'd them a' just ane by ane,
Gude ale keeps my heart aboon

Gude ale hauds me bare and busy,
Gars me moop wi' the servant hizzie,
Stand i' the stool when I hae done,
Gude ale keeps my heart aboon.
O gude ale comes and good ale goes,
Gude ale gars me sell my hose,
Sell my hose, and pawn my shoon,
Gude ale keeps my heart aboon.

'O Gude Ale Comes', Robert Burns, 1795

When Ludwig Zamenhof invented Esperanto in 1887, his goal was for humans to communicate in a common language so peace and international understanding could be fostered regardless of regional or national tongues. Perhaps he was not aware that a lingua franca already existed and it is called beer.

Oh beer, priceless gift to humanity, begetter of happiness, sociability, and companionship. No wonder it is the world's number one favourite alcoholic beverage. And astonishingly it makes number three behind water (number one) and tea (number two) as the most widely and often consumed drinks. Walk past a pub, inn, saloon, tavern, shebeen, bar, café, brasserie, bodega, lodge, boozer, and look at the people who are having the most fun. What are they swigging? Beer, bier, cerveja, biera, ビール, birra, bière, пиво, μπύρα, cerveza, 啤酒 of course!

Beer is the essential social beverage. There is nothing wrong with drinking it alone at home but how much better does it taste when consumed in company? Beer is not the drink to turn to when in shock, or for drowning one's sorrows. Beer is playful. How many times does a quick beer after work end up hours later with people singing, arms round each other, as they profess unending friendship? It is beer goggles that make the world beautiful – not brandy goggles.

Picture the scene. A group of strangers are in a pub. One drinks a whisky, another person a glass of wine; someone orders vodka. Chances are they will remain strangers. Now take that same group and fill their glasses with beer. Within minutes they will be friends. Beer drinking encourages bonhomie. I have the satisfaction of observing this close up because I occasionally take visitors from all over the world around one of Britain's leading breweries. Some speak little or no English. Tour groups vary in their make-up: individuals, couples, sets of work colleagues. People are often shy and don't interact with each other beforehand. But in the bar afterwards when they start drinking the beer, something magical happens. Noise levels increase, laughter punctuates the air, and the atmosphere becomes very jolly as beer breaks down the barriers and everyone starts talking to one another – regardless of mother tongue. Then afterwards, as the visitors leave the bar, faces lit up with smiles, they invariably head to the nearest pub for more beer together with their new pals...

On a recent trip to Zambia, where there are 72 tribal languages, I studied enough of the four main dialects to make myself understood when I ended up in the bar each night to drink Mosi, the local brew. In Zambia I realised that in addition to beer there is another international language – football. Luckily I am fluent in both so now I have new mates in Mongu, Lusaka, and Mufulira. It may have been Wayne Rooney who introduced us but it was beer that sealed our friendship.

Beer O'Clock: Craft, Cask and Culture, Jane Peyton, 2013

Give my people plenty of beer, good beer and cheap beer, and you will have no revolution among them.

Queen Victoria

> *The white sheet bleaching on the hedge,*
> *With heigh! the sweet birds, O, how they sing!*
> *Doth set my pugging tooth on edge;*
> *For a quart of ale is a dish for a king.*
>
> **The Winter's Tale, William Shakespeare, 1623**

Whether Scurvy-grass, Daucus, Gill, Butler, or Broom,
Or from London, or Southwark, or Lambeth we come;
We humbly implore since the Wine in the Nation,
Has of late so much lost its once great Reputation;
That such Liquor as ours which is genuine and true,
And which all our Masters so carefully brew,
Which all men approve of, tho' many drink wine,
Yet the good Oyl of Barly there's none will decline:
That we as a body call'd corp'rate may stand,
And a Patent procure from your Seal and your Hand,
That none without Licence, call'd Special shall fail,
To drink any thing else but Strong Nappy Brown Ale.

The Bacchanalian Sessions: or The Contention of Liquors,
Richard Ames, c. 1663

The first line refers to herbs used as flavourings in beer at a time when the hop was not in universal use.

For decades, the wine trade has been built on education. Those who market wine realised early on that the key to success was to place power in the hands of the consumers. They didn't talk down to them; they didn't take them for granted. Instead, they shared their knowledge. They put information about grapes and techniques and provenance and culture on their bottle labels; they described perfect food pairings; they went out and talked to the customers, offering tasting sessions and explaining all about the product. Customers responded positively. Wine came to be seen as a sophisticated product, something to learn more about. Over time, wine drinkers began to feel that they not only understood the product but also were rather knowledgeable about it. Ringing cash registers testified to a winning formula.

Only in recent years has the beer industry cottoned on to the value of education. Trapped for decades in a race-to-the-bottom cycle of self-deprecation, its business model, on the whole, was based on a combination of patronising, whimsical adverts and rock-bottom prices. No mention was made of how beers were produced beyond the anodyne 'brewed from the finest ingredients'. Brewers, when questioned about their malts and hops, would often decline to answer, citing commercial confidentiality. Finally, the penny dropped. At last, bottle labels began to have something to say. Even the subject of food-pairing raised its head. The industry began to grow up and treat its customers like adults. That we live in such an exciting age for beer must, surely, be partly as a result of this change of emphasis.

Now we need to take things further, to build on what's been achieved and to foster a demanding beer-drinking public that takes pride in its favourite tipple and will push it to ever-greater heights.

So You Want to Be a Beer Expert, Jeff Evans, 2015

Glorious Mild, that Drink Divine,
That Nectar, far surpassing Wine,
That Noble Cordial swill'd by Porters,
And bless'd by Soldiers at their Quarters.

The Hudisbrastick Brewer, **Ned Ward, 1714**

Beer at its best is a reflection of a golden field of barley, a reminder of the rich aroma of a hop garden. Scientists can argue endlessly about the merits of the man-made concoctions which go into much of today's beer but the proof of the pint is in the drinking... the best of British beer is produced from the gifts that nature gave us and by methods which have been proudly handed down over the centuries. The story of beer is a story of nature and of craftsmanship; a story of farmers and brewers who join forces to create beer naturally.

Beer Naturally, **Michael Hardman, 1976**

Michael Hardman MBE is a founder member of CAMRA.

Why, if 'tis dancing you would be,
There's brisker pipes than poetry.
Say, for what were hop-yards meant,
Or why was Burton built on Trent?
Oh many a peer of England brews
Livelier liquor than the Muse,
And malt does more than Milton can
To justify God's ways to man.
Ale, man, ale's the stuff to drink
For fellows whom it hurts to think:
Look into the pewter pot
To see the world as the world's not.
And faith, 'tis pleasant till 'tis past:
The mischief is that 'twill not last.
Oh I have been to Ludlow fair
And left my necktie God knows where,
And carried half way home, or near
Pints and quarts of Ludlow beer:
Then the world seemed none so bad,
And I myself a sterling lad;
And down in lovely muck I've lain,
Happy till I woke again.

A Shropshire Lad, **A. E. Housman, 1896**

Oh, genial and gladdening is the power of good ale, the true
and proper drink of Englishmen! He is not deserving of the
name of Englishman who speaketh against ale

Lavengro, **George Henry Borrow, 1851**

Back and side go bare, go bare;
Both foot and hand go cold:
But belly, God send thee good ale enough,
Whether it be new or old.

I cannot eat but little meat,
My stomach is not good;
But sure I think, that I can drink
With him that wears a hood.
Though I go bare, take ye no care,
I am nothing a-cold;
I stuff my skin so full within
Of jolly good ale and old.

Sixteenth-century English drinking song

This song appears in Gammer Gurton's Needle, *published in 1575 and regarded as one of the earliest comedies in the English language.*

ENJOYING BEER

> I liked the taste of beer, its live, white lather, its brass-bright depths, the sudden world through the wet brown walls of the glass, the tilted rush to the lips and the slow swallowing down to the lapping belly, the salt on the tongue, the foam at the corners.
>
> *Portrait of the Artist as a Young Dog,*
> Dylan Thomas, 1940

In common with the beer-loving Housman's Blue Remembered Hills, *the first taste of beer is never forgotten, even if that first sip was not enjoyed. Graham Greene detested his first acquaintance with English bitter but fortunately – given his family's involvement in brewing – he soon acquired a palate for it. Even in Orwell's dystopian horror of* Nineteen Eighty-Four, *older 'proles' remember the pleasures of beer before Big Brother's dictatorship. On happier grounds, many writers recall fondly the rich flavours and depths of ale and beer, and remind us that beer is a complex beverage: ever since the hop was brought into the brewing process, the end product has been a careful balance of the biscuit and roasted character of grain with the sharp aromas imparted by the hop plant. What some writers in earlier centuries would make of the penchant among some modern brewers to make 'hop-forward' beers is difficult to imagine: these brewers should be reminded that older practitioners of the craft call malt 'the soul of beer', underscored by Housman's edict: 'Malt does more than Milton can/To justify God's way to man'.*

A few mornings after his incarceration, Mr. Samuel Weller, having arranged his master's room with all possible care, and seen him comfortably seated over his books and papers, withdrew to employ himself for an hour or two to come, as he best could. It was a fine morning, and it occurred to Sam that a pint of porter in the open air would lighten his next quarter of an hour or so, as well as any little amusement in which he could indulge.

Having arrived at this conclusion, he betook himself to the tap. Having purchased the beer, and obtained, moreover, the day-but-one-before-yesterday's paper, he repaired to the skittle-ground, and seating himself on a bench, proceeded to enjoy himself in a very sedate and methodical manner.

First of all, he took a refreshing draught of the beer, and then he looked up at a window, and bestowed a Platonic wink on a young lady who was peeling potatoes thereat. Then he opened the paper, and folded it so as to get the police reports outwards; and this being a vexatious and difficult thing to do, when there is any wind stirring, he took another draught of the beer when he had accomplished it. Then, he read two lines of the paper, and stopped short to look at a couple of men who were finishing a game at rackets, which, being concluded, he cried out 'wery good,' in an approving manner, and looked round upon the spectators, to ascertain whether their sentiments coincided with his own. This involved the necessity of looking up at the windows also; and as the young lady was still there, it was an act of common politeness to wink again, and to drink to her good health in dumb show, in another draught of the beer, which Sam did; and having frowned hideously upon a small boy who had noted this latter proceeding with open eyes, he threw one leg over the other, and, holding the newspaper in both hands, began to read in real earnest.

The Pickwick Papers, **Charles Dickens, 1836**

The Rat, meanwhile, was busy examining the label on one of the beer-bottles. 'I perceive this to be Old Burton,' he remarked approvingly. 'SENSIBLE Mole! The very thing! Now we shall be able to mull some ale! Get the things ready, Mole, while I draw the corks.'

It did not take long to prepare the brew and thrust the tin heater well into the red hot heart of the fire; and soon every field-mouse was sipping and coughing and choking (for a little mulled ale goes a long way) and wiping his eyes and laughing and forgetting he had ever been cold in all his life.

The Wind in the Willows, Kenneth Grahame, 1908

When I was sufficiently recovered to be permitted to take some nourishment, I felt the most extraordinary desire for a glass of Guinness, which I knew could be obtained without difficulty. Upon expressing my wish to the doctor, he told me I might take a small glass... It was not long before I sent for the Guinness and I shall never forget how much I enjoyed it. I thought I had never tasted anything so delightful... I am confident that it contributed more than anything else to the renewal of my strength.

From the journal of a British cavalry officer wounded at the Battle of Waterloo, 1815

'Nay, you must have a glass full. It's old ale, such as we don't brew now-a-days; it's as old as Osborne. We brewed it that autumn and we called it the young squire's ale. I though to have tapped it on his marriage, but I don't know when that will come to pass, so we've tapped it now in Roger's honour.'

The old squire had evidently been enjoying the young squire's ale to the verge of prudence. It was indeed as he said, 'as strong as brandy,' and Mr. Gibson had to sip it very carefully as he ate his cold roast beef.

Wives and Daughters, **Elizabeth Gaskell, 1864**

'Then,' said Mr. Codlin, 'fetch me a pint of warm ale, and don't let nobody bring into the room even so much as a biscuit till the time arrives.'

Nodding his approval of this decisive and manly course of procedure, the landlord retired to draw the beer, and presently returning with it, applied himself to warm the same in a small tin vessel shaped funnel-wise, for the convenience of sticking it far down in the fire and getting at the bright places. This was soon done, and he handed it over to Mr. Codlin with that creamy froth upon the surface which is one of the happy circumstances attendant on mulled malt.

The Old Curiosity Shop, **Charles Dickens, 1841**

'I used to go to his house a-courting my first wife, Charlotte, who was his dairymaid. Well, a very good-hearted man were Farmer Everdene, and I being a respectable young fellow was allowed to call and see her and drink as much ale as I liked, but not to carry away any – outside my skin I mane of course.'

'Ay, ay, Jan Coggan; we know yer maning.'

'And so you see 'twas beautiful ale, and I wished to value his kindness as much as I could, and not to be so ill-mannered as to drink only a thimbleful, which would have been insulting the man's generosity...'

'True, Master Coggan, 'twould so,' corroborated Mark Clark.

'... And so I used to eat a lot of salt fish afore going, and then by the time I got there I were as dry as a lime-basket – so thorough dry that that ale would slip down – ah, 'twould slip down sweet! Happy times! heavenly times! Such lovely drunks as I used to have at that house! You can mind, Jacob? You used to go wi' me sometimes.'

'I can – I can,' said Jacob. 'That one, too, that we had at Buck's Head on a White Monday was a pretty tipple.'

Far from the Madding Crowd, **Thomas Hardy, 1874**

Most people hate the taste of beer to begin with. It is, however, a prejudice that many people have been able to overcome.
Winston Churchill

Did you ever taste beer?'

'I had a sip of it once,' said the small servant.

'Here's a state of things!' cried Mr. Swiveller, raising his eyes to the ceiling. 'She never tasted it – it can't be tasted in a sip! Why, how old are you?'

'I don't know.'

Mr. Swiveller opened his eyes very wide, and appeared thoughtful for a moment; then, bidding the child mind the door until he came back, vanished straightaway.

Presently, he returned, followed by the boy from the public-house, who bore in one hand a plate of bread and beef, and in the other a great pot, filled with some very fragrant compound, which sent forth a grateful steam, and was indeed choice purl, made after a particular recipe which Mr. Swiveller had imparted to the landlord, at a period when he was deep in his books and desirous to conciliate his friendship. Relieving the boy of his burden at the door, and charging his little companion to fasten it to prevent surprise, Mr. Swiveller followed her into the kitchen.

'There!' said Richard, putting the plate before her. 'First of all clear that off, and then you'll see what's next.'

The small servant needed no second bidding, and the plate was soon empty.

'Next,' said Dick, handing the purl, 'take a pull at that; but moderate your transports, you know, for you're not used to it. Well, is it good?'

'Oh! isn't it?' said the small servant.

Mr. Swiveller appeared gratified beyond all expression by this reply, and took a long draught himself, steadfastly regarding his companion while he did so.

The Old Curiosity Shop, **Charles Dickens, 1841**

The old man whom he had followed was standing at the bar, having some kind of altercation with the barman, a large, stout, hook-nosed young man with enormous forearms. A knot of others, standing round with glasses in their hands, were watching the scene.

'I arst you civil enough, didn't I?' said the old man, straightening his shoulders pugnaciously. 'You telling me you ain't got a pint mug in the 'ole bleeding boozer?'

'And what in hell's name IS a pint?' said the barman, leaning forward with the tips of his fingers on the counter.

''Ark at 'im! Calls 'isself a barman and don't know what a pint is! Why, a pint's the 'alf of a quart, and there's four quarts to the gallon. 'Ave to teach you the A, B, C next.'

'Never heard of 'em,' said the barman shortly. 'Litre and half litre – that's all we serve. There's the glasses on the shelf in front of you.'

'I likes a pint,' persisted the old man. 'You could 'a drawed me off a pint easy enough. We didn't 'ave these bleeding litres when I was a young man.'

'When you were a young man we were all living in the treetops,' said the barman, with a glance at the other customers.

There was a shout of laughter, and the uneasiness caused by Winston's entry seemed to disappear. The old man's white-stubbled face had flushed pink. He turned away, muttering to himself, and bumped into Winston. Winston caught him gently by the arm. 'May I offer you a drink?' he said.

'You're a gent,' said the other, straightening his shoulders again. He appeared not to have noticed Winston's blue overalls. 'Pint!' he added aggressively to the barman. 'Pint of wallop.'

The barman swished two half-litres of dark-brown beer into thick glasses which he had rinsed in a bucket under the counter. Beer was the only drink you could get in prole pubs. The proles were supposed not to drink gin, though in practice they could get hold of it easily enough. The game of darts was in full swing again, and the knot of men at the bar had begun talking about lottery tickets. Winston's presence was forgotten for a moment. There was a deal table under the window where he and the old man could talk without fear of being overheard. It was horribly dangerous, but at any rate there was no telescreen in the room, a point he had made sure of as soon as he came in.

"E could 'a drawed me off a pint,' grumbled the old man as he settled down behind a glass. 'A 'alf litre ain't enough. It don't satisfy. And a 'ole litre's too much. It starts my bladder running. Let alone the price.'

'You must have seen great changes since you were a young man,' said Winston tentatively.

The old man's pale blue eyes moved from the darts board to the bar, and from the bar to the door of the Gents, as though it were in the bar-room that he expected the changes to have occurred.

'The beer was better,' he said finally. 'And cheaper! When I was a young man, mild beer – wallop we used to call it – was fourpence a pint. That was before the war, of course.'

'Which war was that?' said Winston.

'It's all wars,' said the old man vaguely. He took up his glass, and his shoulders straightened again. "Ere's wishing you the very best of 'ealth!'

Nineteen Eighty-Four, **George Orwell, 1949**

The ale, too – not the modern horror that drives so many men melancholy mad, not the beastliness of these days that makes a fellow's inside like a quaking bog – and as unsteady! Ale that would put the soul of three butchers into one weaver! Ale that would flare like turpentine – genuine Boniface. This immortal viand was vended at two-pence a pint!

The Young Cricketer's Tutor, John Nyren, 1833

John Nyren was the son of Richard Nyren, landlord of the Bat and Ball in Hambledon, Hampshire, in the 18th century. The pub and the cricket ground across the road on Broadhalfpenny Down are commemorated as the cradle of modern cricket. As well running the pub and brewing ale, Richard Nyren helped formulate the rules or 'laws' of the modern game. Hambledon attracted such fine players that the team would take on All England sides. It was at Hambledon that bats became straight rather than curved, the wicket went from two to three stumps and bowling changed from under-arm to over-arm. And prodigious amounts of ale were supped at the pub, which is still open and owned by Fuller's.

Could you imagine a Frenchman, on his own turf, ordering a German wine? Worse still, a French wine pretending to be German? If you could, perhaps you should put your belief to the test. Go to Bordeaux, sit yourself down in a café, bar or restaurant, and say that you fancy a real Blue Nun, so to speak.

Sacre Bleu Soeur! That's fixed you, hasn't it? You have just been on the receiving end of the reaction I suppress every time I see someone who otherwise appears to be British go into his or her local and order something vaguely described as "a lager".

I keep my thoughts to myself because a broken nose would interfere with my appreciation of my superbly aromatic pint of Burton Ale.

Lager has its place. Let us not be niggardly; it has its places. There are at least three of them: Czechoslovakia, if you would like to try the golden-coloured, dry, flowery style of lager that was first made in the town of Pilsen, Bohemia; or Vienna, if you think you might prefer a fuller-coloured, spicier, lager; or Bavaria, if your taste could run to a lager that is sweetly malty and sometimes in the original, dark brown style.

Real lager is dark? I never knew that.

Not many people do, but you won't learn much about lager from drinking the British stuff.

I drink Ersatzenbräu. That's German.

German-ish. It's brewed under licence in a place you thought was nothing more sinister than a missile silo, at a convenient intersection of trucking routes between three major centres of population.

It's modern then, isn't it?

The Bavarians were brewing lager in the 1400s.

It's refreshing. That's really why I drink it.

Ever tried Fuller's Chiswick Bitter in London? Or Jennings' in Cumbria?

Those are beers. I don't like beer.

Lager is beer, too. It is a Bohemian-Austrian-Bavarian style of beer. Ale is a British (and Belgian) style.

Ale? You mean Bitter?

Mild Ale, Bitter Ale, Brown Ale, Pale Ale, Light Ale, Heavy Ale, Old Ale, Barley Wine. Not to mention Porter and Stout...

So this is a question of patriotism?

One reason the French are so keen on their wines is that they have good taste (the people and the claret). Another is that they are proud of the products their country makes best, and put their mouth where their money is.

What does Britain make best?

In the world of beer, we are by far the biggest ale-brewers. With its characteristic fruitiness, fullness of palate, and complexity, ale is to the wold of beer what claret and burgundy are to the universe of wine. Our ales are the clarets of the beer world.

Can you really talk of ale in those terms?

The Belgians put theirs in Champagne bottles, wrap them in tissue paper, lay them down in the cellar, and serve it in Burgundy samplers. The Americans are trying furiously to emulate British ale. Ever come across Ballard Bitter, from Seattle, Washington? Or Big Foot Barley Wine, from Chico, California?

Let's be British about this – and no tissue paper, please. Let's go to a pub.

'But I don't like beer...', Michael Jackson, *Good Beer Guide*, 1988

Alcohol began to appeal to me in the innocent form of bitter beer. I was offered beer first by Lubbock, my riding master, whom I visited one evening in summer. I hated the taste and drank it down with an effort to prove my manliness, and yet some days later, on a long country walk with Raymond, the memory of the taste came back to taunt my thirst. We stopped at an inn for bread and cheese, and I drank bitter for the second time and enjoyed the taste with a pleasure that has never failed me since.

***A Sort of Life*, Graham Greene, 1971**

Graham Greene, as well as being – arguably – the greatest British novelist of the 20th century, was a member of the Greene family that forms the Greene King brewing dynasty in Suffolk. He visited the brewery on a number of occasions to 'start the mash' for special brews.

It was the most beautiful colour that the eye of an artist in beer could desire; full in body, yet brisk as a volcano; piquant, yet without a twang; luminous as an autumn sunset; free from streakiness of taste; but, finally, rather heady. The masses worshipped it, the minor gentry loved it more than wine, and by the most illustrious county families it was not despised. Anybody brought up for being drunk and disorderly in the streets of its natal borough, had only to prove that he was a stranger to the place and its liquor to be honourably dismissed by the magistrates, as one overtaken in a fault that no man could guard against who had entered the town unawares.

The Trumpet Major, **Thomas Hardy, 1880**

Hardy was referring to the beer of Casterbridge, his name for Dorchester. Eldridge Pope, based in Dorchester, created Thomas Hardy's Ale, a 12 per cent bottle-conditioned beer, in his memory. When the brewery closed, a few smaller breweries attempted to produce the beer but its long method of production and maturation disrupted their regular beers. At the time of writing, an Italian company is attempting to relaunch it.

Have you ever had that moment when you smell the perfume or cologne of a long-lost love and you smile, just a little bit, to yourself as long-buried memories bubble to the surface?

I say this because, not so long ago, I had a powerful reminder that taking the time to smell the beer (or the roses for that matter) shouldn't only be about letting you know it's free of faults and drinkable, it should also help you capture moments that you're enjoying with friends and loved ones.

I say this with conviction because I experienced 'smell recall' recently when the mere act of opening a little wooden box led to the unearthing of a memory that was so joyous, so visceral, that it bought tears to my eyes and a huge smile to my lips.

It was a memory of my Granddad, Alf Cole, who was a man I loved dearly. In fact, I'd go as far to say idolised. He died when I was 12 and, to this day, I find it heart-breaking he didn't live to see me grow up; I hope he would have been proud of me but, if nothing else, he would have enjoyed more than his share of free beer, that's for sure!

But what was it that unleashed this tidal wave of emotions? It was actually the mundane action of opening a little box where I keep little mementos of things like concert or cricket match stubs, a rosary my grandmother gave me and a few other bits and bobs.

So, despite having opened it hundreds of times, when I lifted the lid and the box wafted its muted sandalwood scent at me, powerful memories were unleashed and I was transported back at least 30 years to a bright summer's day in the Barley Mow pub garden on idyllic Englefield Green in Surrey and my Granddad holding his pint glass to my lips for me to take an illicit sip, which I'm pretty sure is my earliest beer-related memory – but it's so much more than that.

With that aroma came a host of other remembered scents – over the pungent nuttiness of the beer, I could smell the smoke on his fingers, the Brylcream in his hair and, throughout, the woody note from the Old Spice shaving cream that he used, whisking it to a lather in its branded china pot with a badger hair brush.

I then remembered how I would find him in the morning, carefully shaving in a mirror at the kitchen sink because it had the best light, wearing just his vest and trousers, with his braces flapping around the backs of his legs; how he'd pretend I wasn't there as he carefully finished, then wiping any excess foam away before giving me a good morning kiss and making me my breakfast, which was always a bowl of cornflakes followed by blackcurrant jam on toast – the latter of which I still love to this day.

I feel so privileged to have these precious memories gifted back to me for the rest of my life by the simple act of opening a wooden box that I just want to encourage you to stop and smell the beer when you're enjoying yourself and hopefully, one day, the smell of a pint will make you as happy as this experience did me.

Let Me Tell You About Beer, **Melissa Cole, 2014**

*A fine beer may be judged with only one sip,
but it is better to be thoroughly sure.*
Czech proverb

ON THE ROAD

I rose politely in the club
And said "I feel a little bored;
Will someone take me to a pub?"

'A Ballade of an Anti-Puritan',
G.K. Chesterton, 1916

Inns are deeply embedded in the folklore of Britain. They have stood for centuries, offering travellers, on foot, coach, train or car, a welcome that combines warmth, food and drink. Neil Hanson's evocative description of the Tan Hill Inn atop the raw, blustery Pennines brings to life a hostelry that existed before the Roman invasion of the British Isles. Chaucer's famous pilgrims made their way to Canterbury via a succession of inns and taverns where comfortable beds were as important as flowing tankards and groaning platters. In the great age of the coach, many writers, with Dickens and Dr Johnson to the fore, journeyed extensively by horse-drawn conveyance and vividly described the pleasures of their accommodation in roadside inns, often in bleak terrain.

When the 'iron horse' replaced the four-legged variety, new inns, often with 'railway' in their names, were built to greet travellers who could cover the country in a few hours rather than several days. But, as the imposing George in Stamford proves, the days of great coaching inns are not forgotten.

> In Southwerk at the Tabard as I lay
> Redy to wenden on my pilgrymage
> To Caunterbury with ful devout corage,
> At nyght was come into that hostelrye
> Wel nyne and twenty in a compaignye
> Of sondry folk, by aventure yfalle
> In felaweshipe, and pilgrimes were they alle,
> That toward Caunterbury wolden ryde.
> The chambres and the stables weren wyde,
> And wel we weren esed atte beste;
> And shortly, whan the sonne was to reste,
> So hadde I spoken with hem everichon
> That I was of hir felaweshipe anon,
> And made forward erly for to ryse
> To take our wey, ther as I yow devyse.

The Canterbury Tales, Geoffrey Chaucer, 1475

The Tabard in Southwark, on the outskirts of London, was a popular departure point for the pilgrimage to Canterbury. The Canterbury Tales' *narrator describes meeting with a group of 29 'sundry folk' staying at the Tabard and arranging to travel in their company.*

At length, he drove leisurely to London on the third day... *He*, I promise, did not decline the obsequious invitation of the landlords to alight and refresh himself in the neat country towns. Having partaken of a copious breakfast, with fish, and rice, and hard eggs, at Southampton, he had so far rallied at Winchester as to think a glass of sherry necessary. At Alton he stepped out of the carriage at his servant's request and imbibed some of the ale for which the place is famous. At Farnham he stopped to view the Bishop's Castle, and to partake of a light dinner of stewed eels, veal cutlets, and French beans, with a bottle of claret... when he drove into town he was as full of wine, beer, meat, pickles, cherry-brandy, and tobacco as the steward's cabin of a steam-packet.

Vanity Fair, **William Makepeace Thackeray, 1848**

The good stabling and the good ale of the Mariners, though somewhat difficult to reach on account of there being but this narrow way to both, were nevertheless perseveringly sought out by the sagacious old heads who knew what was what in Casterbridge.

The Mayor of Casterbridge, Thomas Hardy, 1886

As we came further north the mire grew deeper. About eight o'clock it began to fall heavily, and, as we crossed the wild heaths hereabout, there was no vestige of a track. The mail kept on well, however, and at eleven we reached a bare place with a house standing alone in the midst of a dreary moor, which the guard informed us was Greta Bridge. I was in a perfect agony of apprehension, for it was fearfully cold, and there were no outward signs of anybody being up in the house. But to our great joy we discovered a comfortable room, with drawn curtains and a most blazing fire. In half an hour they gave us a smoking supper and a bottle of mulled port (in which we drank your health), and then we retired to a couple of capital bedrooms, in each of which there was a rousing fire halfway up the chimney.

We had for breakfast, toast, cakes, a Yorkshire pie, a piece of beef about the size and much the shape of my portmanteau, tea, coffee, ham, and eggs; and are now going to look about us.

Charles Dickens in a letter to his wife, 1838

Charles Dickens travelled north by mail coach to research conditions in Yorkshire schools. Here he recounts his reception at the New Inn, cast as the George and New Inn in Nicholas Nickleby.

The day dragged on uncomfortably enough, and about six o'clock that night he and Mr. Squeers, and the little boys, and their united luggage, were all put down together at the George and New Inn, Greta Bridge.

Mr. Squeers, being safely landed, left Nicholas and the boys standing with the luggage in the road, to amuse themselves by looking at the coach as it changed horses, while he ran into the tavern and went through the leg-stretching process at the bar. After some minutes he returned with his legs thoroughly stretched, if the hue of his nose and a short hiccup afforded any criterion.

Nicholas Nickleby, **Charles Dickens, 1838**

Lincolnshire is fertile territory for coaching inns thanks to its proximity to the Great North Way. The George [in Stamford], with its famous 'gallows' inn sign that stretches across the road, is just one of 400 listed buildings in this breathtaking town of mellow stone where *Middlemarch* was filmed for television.

The inn dates from 947 when monks were said to have built a hostelry on the site. The present site developed from three medieval buildings: the House of the Holy Sepulchre, a monastic hospice where the Knights of St John were entertained before starting their journey to the Holy Land; a church; and the Hospital of St John and St Thomas, founded in 1174 for the poor of Peterborough. The present site was built in 1597 for the first Baron Burghley, Elizabeth I's chief minister, who ordered the execution of Mary Queen of Scots.

Charles I stayed at the inn on several occasions, the last in 1645 when, disguised as a servant, he fled from Oxford and spent his last night as a free man at Stamford before joining the Scottish army at Newark. He was captured and handed over to Oliver Cromwell's forces and remained under arrest until his trial and execution.

In its heyday as a coaching inn, the George served '20 up and 20 down' a day, a reference to the direction in which the coaches were travelling. At each side of the stone-flagged hall are the London and York rooms, named after the destinations of the coaches, which stopped at the inn to change horses. Among the many famous guests at the George was Daniel Lambert, who died in Stamford in 1809 aged 32 and weighing 52 stones, eleven pounds. The lobby of the George has a portrait of him and the great walking stick used to balance his enormous frame.

Britain's 500 Best Pubs, **Roger Protz, 2000**

One of the oldest inns on the road was the Old Angel at Doncaster, which was connected with coaching from its introduction to its fall, and when stage coaching fell this celebrated old posting house fell with it. Royalty on several occasions honoured it with their presence. In 1603 James I stayed within its walls, while in 1778 His Royal Highness the Duke of York remained at least one night, and a week later the Prince of Wales was an occupant of the state rooms; both rested here on their return journey in the same month; and the Duke of York again slept here in 1759, whilst noblemen and gentlemen innumerable availed themselves of its excellent accommodation.

Mr Woodcock was the next landlord of the Angel, and he was at the house and had charge of mails when the first Mail coach came along the road in 1786. This coach, nevertheless, was worked from the Red Lion, in Scot Lane, which at that time was a coaching house. The major and corporation seemed to have 'kept it up' pretty considerably in those days, as we find their names and the Angel in constant collision, and some of our municipal ratepayers would open their eyes if they found such items paid out of the rates as: the ringers when the Marquess of Rockingham dined at the Angel, £1; the waits playing at the Angel, 5s; to extra music at the Angel during Alderman Whitaker's year of office, £6 6s; to say nothing of the various sums voted for sack and brisket, and we can now easily understand the source of inspiration which prompted the following:

The Doncaster mayor sits in his chair,
His mills they merrily go,
His nose doth shine with drinking wine,
And the gout is in his great toe.

The Old Coaching Days in Yorkshire, Tom Bradley, 1988

11th (Thursday)... we were carried out of our way to a town where we would lye, since we could not go so far as we would. And there with great difficulty come about ten at night to a little inn [George, Salisbury], where we were fain to go into a room where a pedlar was in bed, and made him rise; and there wife and I lay, and in a truckle-bed Betty Turner and Willett. But good beds, and the master of the house a sober, understanding man, and I had a discourse with him about this country's matters, as wool and corne, and other things. And he also merry, and made us mighty merry at supper... By and by to bed, glad of this mistake, because, it seems, had we gone on as we intended, we could not have passed with our coach, and must have lain on the Plain all night...

12th (Friday). Up, finding our beds good but lousy; which made us merry. We set out, the reckoning and the servants coming to 9s. 6d.

The Diary of Samuel Pepys, 1668

It was on the great northern road from York to London, about the beginning of the month of October, and about the hour of eight in the evening, that four travellers were, by a violent shower of rain, driven for shelter into a little public-house on the side of the highway, distinguished by a sign which was said to exhibit the figure of a black lion. The kitchen, in which they were assembled, was the only room for entertainment in the house, paved with red bricks, remarkably clean, furnished with three or four Windsor chairs, adorned with shining plates of pewter, and copper saucepans nicely scoured, that even dazzled the eyes of the beholder; while a cheerful fire of sea-coal blazed in the chimney.

The Adventures of Sir Lancelot Greaves,
Tobias Smollett, 1762

How fine it is to enter some old town, walled and turreted, just at approach of night-fall, or to come to some straggling village, with the lights streaming through the surrounding gloom; and then, after inquiring for the best entertainment that the place affords, to 'take one's ease at one's inn!'

'On Going on a Journey', William Hazlitt, 1822

We dined at an excellent inn at Chapel-house, where he expatiated on the felicity of England in its taverns and inns, and triumphed over the French for not having, in any perfection, the tavern life. 'There is no private house, (said he), in which people can enjoy themselves so well, as at a capital tavern... at a tavern, there is general freedom from anxiety. You are sure you are welcome: and the more noise you make, the more trouble you give, the more good things you call for, the welcome you are... No, sir; there is nothing which has yet been contrived by man, by which so much happiness is produced as by a good tavern or inn.' He then repeated, with great emotion, Shenstone's lines:

> *'Whoe'er has travel'd life's dull round,*
> *Where'er his stages may have been,*
> *May sigh to think he still has found*
> *The warmest welcome at an inn.'*

The Life of Samuel Johnson, James Boswell, 1776

Tan Hill sits right on the Pennine Way, at the crossroads of tracks that were ancient when the Romans invaded Britain. Drovers, pack-horse traders and the coal miners who worked the numerous fell-top pits all once used the inn. There is nothing luxurious about Tan Hill's thick stone walls, flagged floors and wooden benches, but countless lost and weary travellers down the centuries have been grateful for the shelter offered by this lonely inn, and for the warmth from its blazing open fire. Now it sits in splendid isolation, its nearest neighbour almost four miles away, the only sounds the bleating of sheep, the call of grouse and curlew and the wind keening across the moor.

The wind blows so strongly here that many incautious motorists have lost their car doors to it – one famous landlady declared that it blew hard enough to 'blow the horns off a tup' (the local word for a ram) – and in winter it can whip the snow up into huge drifts that block the inn off from the outside world for weeks at a time.

A tale is told of the landlord who wished a shepherd 'Happy New Year' on 16 April because he was the first person he had seen that year. In another winter it was so cold that the whisky froze in the optics behind the bar! The Swaledale breed of sheep, with their distinctive black faces and white noses, was developed in the area around Tan Hill, and they are so hardy that they live up on 'the tops' in all but the wildest weather and can survive on a diet that would starve almost any other breed. If buried under snow they have been known to survive for weeks, even eating their own fleeces to do so.

Tan Hill's isolation is lessened by the annual influx of summer tourists, and on the last Thursday in May every year it plays host to the Swaledale sheep world championship – the Tan Hill Show. On that day, a thousand people will be there to look at the sheep or just to share in the atmosphere of a unique event – there is no other country show like it. The judging of the sheep is deadly serious – a champion tup can command a price of well into five figures – and the judges' decisions will be discussed and disputed far into the night. The uninvolved can simply sit outside on a warm spring evening and listen as the sound of a silver band playing the local anthem 'Beautiful Swaledale' drifts over the fells.

The Tan Hill is absolutely unique. See it in summer, surrounded by ten thousand acres of moorland. In winter snows it is best to leave it to the sheep and the shepherds who have learned to live with its wild weather – if you are lucky you may be stranded in the inn for some weeks and will have some tales to tell your friends; but if you are not so lucky, you may be dead from exposure before help can reach you.

Classic Country Pubs, Neil Hanson, 1987

Neil Hanson, a former editor of CAMRA's Good Beer Guide, *loves the Tan Hill Inn so much that he has twice managed the pub. He records his memories in two books,* The Inn at the Top *and* Pigs Might Fly.

PORTER

Porter was a style of beer developed early in the 18th century that dramatically changed brewing. It was first produced in London but its impact spread beyond the British Isles. Porter brewing coincided with the first stirrings of the industrial revolution, with London changing into a large city with many thirsty workers. Early in the 18th century a beer that was a mix of pale, brown and 'stale' [old] ales became popular. To avoid having to blend three beers, brewers produced a beer served from one cask or butt that replicated the flavours of the mixture known as three threads or three thirds. Brewers called the new beer entire butt, as it came from one cask, but it quickly acquired the name of porter as a result of its popularity with the section of the working population that included porters who worked in the markets and docks.

Porter's popularity was such that brewers such as Samuel Whitbread produced more than 100,000 barrels a year of Porter and its stronger version stout porter – later shortened to just stout. Porter brewers engaged in grandiose promotions for their products. A dinner at Thrale's Anchor Brewery in

Southwark took place inside a new porter vat and was attended by Sir Joshua Reynolds, Dr Samuel Johnson, Oliver Goldsmith and David Garrick. Meux built a vat measuring 60 feet wide and 23 feet high and in 1795 added another vat that held 20,000 barrels of beer. This chest-puffing only ended when disaster struck Meux's brewery in Tottenham Court Road and a porter vat burst, killing and injuring many bystanders.

The popularity of porter and stout declined in the 19th century as Victorian drinkers switched to a maltier, less bitter beer called mild. But the style remained much in evidence, and was mentioned by Dickens and Tennyson.

The production of porter and stout came to a halt during World War One when the government banned brewers from using heavily roasted malt that needed too much energy in the form of coal, gas and electricity, all of which were directed to the manufacture of armaments. As a result, porter and stout production became an Irish speciality. Guinness flourished to such an extent that it was for a period the biggest brewery in the world.

In Ireland, porter was called 'plain', its casks branded with a single X, while stout casks carried XX. Dublin plain became an institution. But as a result of increases in beer duty in the 20th century, XX stout and X plain were reduced in strength and porter went into slow and then terminal decline. But it was not forgotten.

> Harwood my townsman, he invented first,
> Porter to rival wine and quench the thirst.
> Porter which spreads itself half the world o'er,
> Whose reputation rises more and more.
> As long as porter shall preserve its fame
> Let all with gratitude our Parish name.
> **The Gentleman's Magazine, 1819**

According to this piece of doggerel by a man called Gutteridge, a brewer in Shoreditch called Ralph Harwood was the first porter brewer. Harwood certainly brewed porter but there's no evidence he was the first to make it.

> A poet, starving in a Garret
> Conning old Topicks like a Parrot,
> Invokes his Mistress and his Muse,
> And stays at home for Want of Shoes:
> Should but his Muse descending drop
> A slice of Bread and Mutton-Chop;
> Or kindly when his Credit's out
> Surprise him with a pint of Stout.
> **'Poem to Stella', Jonathan Swift, 1720**

The Irish poet and satirist Jonathan Swift, living in London, extolled the virtues of stout.

Would you believe it, although water is to be had in abundance in London and of fairly good quality, absolutely none is drunk? The lower classes, even the paupers, do not know what it is to quench their thirst with water. In this country nothing but beer is drunk and it is made in several qualities. Small beer is what everyone drinks when thirsty; it is used even in the best houses and costs only a penny a pot. Another kind of beer is called porter, meaning carrier, because the greater quantity of this beer is consumed by the working classes. It is a thick and strong beverage, and the effect it produces if drunk in excess is the same as that of wine; this porter costs threepence the pot. In London there are a number of ale-houses where nothing but this sort of beer sold. There are again other clear beers, called ale, some of these being as transparent as fine old wine, foreigners often mistaking them at first sight for the latter. The prices of ales differ, some costing one shilling the bottle, and others as much as eighteen pence. It is said that more grain is consumed in England for making beer than for making bread.

A foreign view of England in the reigns of George I & George II,
César de Saussure, 1726

César de Saussure was a young Swiss man who left home in 1725 and travelled Europe for eleven years, recounting his experiences and observations in letters to his family.

> *Beer, commonly call'd Porter, is almost become the universal Cordial of the Populace, especially since the necessary Period of prohibiting the Corn Distillery; the Suppression presently advanc'd the Price of that common Poison Gin, to near three times its former Price and the consumption of beer has kept pace with such advance.*
>
> **Essay on Bread, H Jackson, 1758**

> Brewers pining at the hardships they labour under and rolling away in their coaches and six [horses] to their several villas to drown their grief in burgundy and champaign.
>
> **The Gentleman's Magazine, 1762**

The London porter brewers amassed considerable wealth and as a result were given the nickname of 'the Beerage'. The porter brewers often complained of their long working hours, which drew this response from the Gentleman's Magazine.

To the Meux family goes the dubious honour of having built the largest porter vat of the 18th century. *The Times* of the 7th of April, 1785, reported the construction: 'There is a cask now building at Messrs Meux and Co's brewery in Lickapond Street, Grays Inn Lane, the size of which exceeds all credibility, being designed to hold 20,000 barrels of Porter. The whole expense attending the same will be upwards of £10,000'.

In October, 1814, owing to the defective state of its hoops, it burst and the results were most disastrous. The brewery in Tottenham Court Road was at that time hemmed in by miserable tenements which were crowded by people of the poorer classes. Some of these houses were simply flooded with Porter; two or three collapsed and no less than eight persons met their death either in the ruins, or from drowning, the fumes of the Porter or by drunkenness. At the inquest the jury returned the verdict: death by casualty.

The Curiosities of Ale & Beer, John Bickerdyke, 1889

And hence this halo lives about
The waiter's hands, that reach
To each his perfect pint of stout,
His proper chop to each.

'Will Waterproof's Lyrical Monologue',
Alfred, Lord Tennyson, 1842

The reputation and enjoyment of London porter is by no means confined to England; as a proof of the truth of this assertion, this house exports annually very large quantities; so far extended are its commercial connections that Thrale's intire is well known, as a delicious beverage, from the frozen regions of Russia to the burning sands of Bengal and Sumatra. The empress of all Russia, is, indeed, so partial to porter that she has ordered repeatedly very large quantities for her own drinking and that of her court.

The History and Antiquities of the Parish of St Saviour,
Southwark, Matthew Concanen Jr, Aaron Morgan, 1795

The London brewers were keen exporters of porter and stout. Supplies went to Ireland, mainland Europe, the Baltic States, the Caribbean, the Far East and the Americas.

When the sale of Thrale's brewery was going forward, Johnson appeared bustling about, with an inkhorn and pen in his buttonhole, like an exciseman; and on being asked what he really considered to be the value of the property which was to be disposed of, answered, 'We are not here to sell a parcel of boilers and vats, but the potentiality of growing rich beyond the dreams of avarice.'

The Life of Samuel Johnson, **James Boswell, 1781**

The lexicographer and writer Dr Samuel Johnson lived with the Thrale family. When Henry Thrale died in 1781, Johnson was one of the executors of the will.

'You see how these fellows drink, and smoke, and roar,' replied
Mr. Pickwick. 'It's quite impossible that they can mind
it much.'

'Ah, that's just the very thing, sir,' rejoined Sam, 'they don't
mind it; it's a regular holiday to them – all porter and skittles.
It's t'other vuns as gets done over, vith this sort of thing: them
down-hearted fellers as can't svig away at the beer, nor play at
skittles neither.'

The Pickwick Papers, **Charles Dickens, 1836**

We sat in Grogan's with our faded overcoats finely disarrayed
on easy chairs in the mullioned snug. I gave a shilling and two
pennies to a civil man who brought us in return two glasses
of black porter, imperial pint measure. I adjusted the glasses
to the front of each of us and reflected on the solemnity of
the occasion. It was my first taste of porter...

The porter was sour to the palate, but viscid, potent. Kelly
made a long noise as if releasing air from his interior.

I looked at him from the corner of my eye and said:

'You can't beat a good pint!'

He leaned over and put his face close to me in an earnest
manner.

'Do you know what I am going to tell you,' he said, with his
wry mouth, 'a pint of plain is your only man.'

At Swim-Two-Birds, **Flann O'Brien, 1939**

THIS IS THE FIRST ADVERTISEMENT EVER ISSUED

in a national paper
to advertise

GUINNESS

For over 150 years the House of Guinness have been engaged in brewing Stout. By concentrating upon doing one thing well, they have produced a beverage which stands alone.

Fortunes have been spent in study and development, going right back to the production of the kind of Barley seed that will enable the farmers to grow the Barley that makes the most suitable malt to make the best Stout.

As a result of quality, and quality alone, the Guinness Brewery has grown to be far the largest in the world

ITS GREAT PURITY

Guinness is made solely from Barley, Malt, Hops and Yeast, and is naturaly matured. No artificial colour is added; the colour of Guinness is due to the roasting of the Barley.

ITS HEALTHGIVING VALUE

Guinness builds strong muscles. It feeds exhausted nerves. It enriches the blood. Doctors affirm that Guinness is a valuable restorative after Influenza and other weakening illnesses. Guinness is a valuable natural aid in cases of insomnia.

ITS NOURISHING PROPERTIES

Guinness is one of the most nourishing beverages, richer in carbo-hydrates than a glass of milk. This is one reason why it is so good when people are tired or exhausted.

GUINNESS
IS GOOD FOR YOU

The celebrated advertising line Guinness is Good for You is thought to have been written by the mystery writer Dorothy L Sayers when she was working as a copy writer for a London advertising agency. Brewers are no longer allowed to suggest that beer might be advantageous to health.

When things go wrong and will not come right,
Though you do the best you can,
When life looks black as the hour of night –
A PINT OF PLAIN IS YOUR ONLY MAN.

When money's tight and is hard to get
And your horse has also ran,
When all you have is a heap of debt –
A PINT OF PLAIN IS YOUR ONLY MAN.

When health is bad and your heart feels strange,
And your face is pale and wan,
When doctors say that you need a change,
A PINT OF PLAIN IS YOUR ONLY MAN.

When food is scarce and your larder bare
And no rashers grease your pan,
When hunger grows as your meals are rare –
A PINT OF PLAIN IS YOUR ONLY MAN.

In time of trouble and lousy strife,
You have still got a darlint plan,
You still can turn to a brighter life –
A PINT OF PLAIN IS YOUR ONLY MAN.

At Swim-Two-Birds, **Flann O'Brien, 1939**

'Open two bottles of stout, Jack,' said Mr. O'Connor.

'How can I?' said the old man, 'when there's no corkscrew?'

'Wait now, wait now!' said Mr. Henchy, getting up quickly. 'Did you ever see this little trick?'

He took two bottles from the table and, carrying them to the fire, put them on the hob. Then he sat down again by the fire and took another drink from his bottle...

In a few minutes an apologetic 'Pok!' was heard as the cork flew out of Mr. Lyons' bottle. Mr. Lyons jumped off the table, went to the fire, took his bottle and carried it to the table.

Dubliners, James Joyce, 1914

James Joyce discovered there could be problems enjoying Dublin stout when bottles were sealed with driven corks.

Terence O'Ryan heard him and straightaway brought him a crystal cup full of the foaming ebon ale which the noble twin brothers Bungiveagh and Bungardilaun brew ever in their divine alevats, cunning as the sons of deathless Leda. For they garner the succulent berries of the hop and mass and sift and bruise and brew them and they mix therewith sour juices and bring the must to the sacred fire and cease not night or day from their toil, those cunning brothers, lords of the vat.

Then did you, chivalrous Terence, hand forth, as to the manor born, that nectarous beverage and you offered the crystal cup to him that thirsted, the soul of chivalry, in beauty akin to the immortals.

Ulysses, James Joyce, 1922

Eight years later, Joyce's prose style was more elaborate but his devotion to Dublin beer is still evident.

THE PALE ALE
REVOLUTION

O Beer! O Hodgson, Guinness, Allsopp, Bass!
Names that should be on every infant's tongue!

'Beer', Charles Stuart Calverley, 1862

Porter and stout created a commercial brewing industry in the British Isles but it was the development of pale ale that revolutionised beer-making on a world scale. The success of pale ale and India pale ale was so profound that it influenced the first producers of golden lager in Germany and Bohemia. The first beers fashioned for the India trade were produced in London, with Hodgson at Bow Bridge the main practitioner. But it was Burton upon Trent in the Midlands that became famous as the home of pale ale.

The India trade restored the fortunes of the Burton brewers. Within a few years, sales of beer from Allsopp, Bass, Salt and Worthington rapidly eclipsed those of Hodgson. Bass rose to become the pre-eminent brewer in the town. By the late 1870s, the firm was producing 830,000 barrels a year and that figure rose to one million by the end of the century. Bass became a cult beer both at home and abroad.

From taps in the squares, the beer runs away by a trough into the 'Union-room' – so called because the rows of barrels which are marshalled on its floor are linked together, or 'united', by one pipe.

What a ball-room would this Union-room make if its floor were clear, for it is 125 yards long by as many wide. But instead of dancers it holds 2,500 casks, each one containing 160 gallons. These are ranged in double rows, and above each row is a shallow trough, called the 'barm trough'. Into it flows the beer, and from it, by the removal of plugs, into the casks. It is in these casks, which are fixtures, that the process of fermentation is completed. From each rises an inverted syphon, whose orifice overhangs the 'barm trough. Drip, drip, drip, the yeast – the product of fermentation – comes in frothy clots and glutinous gouts out from the casks by letting in beer from the 'union pipes', whence the room takes its name. The desiderated coolness is maintained while the fermentation is working itself out by cold water contained in a tube which passes through each cask. When all fermentation has ceased – generally the beer is in the 'union casks' from two to three days – it is run off into the racking-room below, where the service or 'trade' casks are at once filled.

A Glass of Pale Ale and a Visit to Burton, **1880**

This unsigned article, first published in the Daily News *in 1872, gives a graphic account of brewing at Bass, showing how the industrial revolution had reshaped industry. The writer described cooling the hopped wort and starting fermentation in open square vessels. Once fermentation was underway, the liquid was transferred to vessels known as 'unions' that were responsible for the singular character of Burton-brewed pale ales. The union room system is still used by Marston's in Burton.*

Alfred, Lord Tennyson, during a public performance of one of his poems at the opening of the 1862 International Exhibition at Crystal Palace.

As I rode down the grassy slopes, I saw coming towards me in the distance the figure of a solitary horseman. It was Younghusband's native servant. At that moment I would have given a kingdom, not for champagne or hock and soda, or hot coffee, but for a glass of beer. He approached and salaamed. I uttered but one word: 'Beer!' Without a moment's hesitation, he put his hand in the fold of his tunic and drew therefrom a bottle of Bass. Happy forethought! O Prince of hosts! Most glorious moment!

Leaves from a Viceroy's Notebook,
George Nathaniel Curzon, 1926

Lord Curzon, Viceroy of India from 1899 to 1905, recalled the time he was trekking from Afghanistan to India on horseback and was greeted by a servant with a bottle of Bass.

'How much Bass wid the label did that ravin' child dhrink?'
'Tain't Bass,' said Ortheris. 'It's a bitterer beer nor that. It's
'ome-sickness!'

'The Madness of Private Ortheris', Rudyard Kipling, 1887

Bass was drunk by the homesick Privates in India, in Kipling's short stories.

'Let's have filleted steak and a bottle of Bass for dinner tonight.
It will be simply exquisite. I shall love it.'
  'But my dear Nella,' he exclaimed, 'steak and beer at Felix's!
It's impossible! Moreover, young women still under twenty-
three cannot be permitted to drink Bass.'

***The Grand Babylon Hotel*, Arnold Bennett, 1902**

As the novelist Arnold Bennett recorded, beer in Edwardian England was not considered suitable for all members of society nor upmarket restaurants.

BREWING
BEER

Just now I have beer in my very soul. The grand object of my ambition is to stand and be fumigated by the smoke of my own vats. It is a fat, prosperous, money-making business, and one in which there is a clear line between right and wrong. No man brews bad beer without knowing it, – or sells short measure. Whether the fatness and the honesty can go together; – that is a problem I want to solve.

Rachel Ray, Anthony Trollope, 1863

Since the earliest days of commercial brewing, people have been keen to make beer, either from a desire to grow rich or out of a passion for the end product. Dickens' hapless Mr Micawber failed to enter any of the portals of the great London breweries but, even though they lacked his financial acumen, they continued on their paths to glory. As the vivid description of Whitbread's porter brewery in London shows, the brewers of the 18th and 19th centuries grasped all the new technologies made available by the industrial revolution to improve the quality of their beers and the methods used to make them.

The rise of big commercial companies, however, sent both publican-brewers and small house breweries into rapid decline, as Dickens' description of the closed brewery at Miss

Havisham's dwelling in Great Expectations *graphically shows. The 19th and 20th centuries were a time of rapid change and development in brewing, but many British brewers remained proudly wedded to traditional methods, none more so than Marston's in the brewing capital of Burton upon Trent with its dedication to the 'Burton union' system of fermentation.*

But until the arrival of CAMRA and a consumer demand for more information about how beer was made and the ingredients used, brewing remained a closed industry. It took the pioneering writing of Frank Baillie to unlock such closely guarded secrets as barley, hops and alcohol strength.

The range of beer brewed today would leave older breweries gasping in disbelief. For years, cask beer meant mild and bitter. But as Adrian Tierney-Jones shows in Britain's Beer Revolution, *the new generation of craft or artisan brewers are a restless crowd, endlessly seeking new styles with the use of New World hops and presenting drinkers with an amazing diversity of aromas, flavours and colours.*

'I will not conceal from you, my dear Mr. Copperfield,' said
Mrs. Micawber, 'that I have long felt the Brewing business to
be particularly adapted to Mr. Micawber. Look at Barclay and
Perkins! Look at Truman, Hanbury and Buxton! It is on that
extensive footing that Mr. Micawber, I know from my own
knowledge of him, is calculated to shine; and the profits, I am
told, are e-NOR-MOUS! But if Mr. Micawber cannot get into
those firms – which decline to answer his letters, when he
offers his services even in an inferior capacity – what is the
use of dwelling upon that idea? None.'

David Copperfield, **Charles Dickens, 1850**

Mr Whitbread's brewery in Chiswell Street, near Moorfields,
is the greatest in London. The commodity produced in it is
also esteemed to be of the best quality of any brewed in the
metropolis. The quantity of porter brewed in the year in this
house is generally about 200,000 barrels.

There is one stone cistern that contains 3,600 barrels, and
there are 49 large oak vats, some of which contain 3,500
barrels... There are three boilers, each of which holds about
500 barrels... In the upper part of the building are cooling
cisterns, that would cover about five acres of land, only six
inches deep, but made quite tight, and kept very clean...

Great improvements are daily making, and particularly in
the boilers. Two of which are covered so as to collect the steam,
and use it instead of cold water, which saves a great deal of
fuel. The barrels or casks, of ordinary dimensions, are in
number about 20,000; 200 workmen are employed, and
80 horses of a very large size. One was lately killed, being
diseased, whose four shoes weighed 24lbs...

In the course of the operations, the beer is forced by a pump, in pipes under the street, to a large building on the other side, to be put in casks. In the mash-tubs which are about 20ft deep, there is a machine to stir up the malt, that constantly turns round, and is very ingeniously managed so by means of a screw, as to rise and fall alternately, so as to move alternately at the top, in the middle and the bottom. Whether the great size, or ingenuity of contrivance is considered, this brewery is one of the greatest curiosities that is to be seen anywhere, and certainly little less than half a million sterling is employed in machinery, buildings and materials. We must not omit here to mention, in contradiction to a long but ill-founded belief, that Thames water alone would make good porter, that in this large brewery the water used is not from the Thames, but from the New River.

The Union Magazine and Imperial Register, **1802**

Brewing stopped at Chiswell Street in 1976 but the Grade II-listed building can be visited. It is used today for conferences and weddings, with events held in the Porter Tun Room, the Sugar Room and The Vaults.

The accommodation of the Three Mariners was far from spacious, despite the fair area of ground it covered. The room demanded by intrusive beams and rafters, partitions, passages, staircases, disused ovens, settles, and four-posters, left comparatively small quarters for human beings. Moreover, this being at a time before home-brewing was abandoned by the smaller victuallers, and a house in which the twelve-bushel strength was still religiously adhered to by the landlord in his ale, the quality of the liquor was the chief attraction of the premises, so that everything had to make way for the utensils and operations in connection therewith.

The Mayor of Casterbridge, **Thomas Hardy, 1886**

One afternoon in late February a warm, rich, appetising scent, such as the animals had never smelt before, wafted itself across the yard from the little brew-house, which had been disused in Jones's time, and which stood beyond the kitchen. Someone said it was the smell of cooking barley. The animals sniffed the air hungrily and wondered whether a warm mash was being prepared for their supper. But no warm mash appeared, and on the following Sunday it was announced that from now onwards all barley would be reserved for the pigs. The field beyond the orchard had already been sown with barley. And the news soon leaked out that every pig was now receiving a ration of a pint of beer daily, with half a gallon for Napoleon himself, which was always served to him in the Crown Derby soup tureen.

Animal Farm, **George Orwell, 1945**

To be sure, it was a deserted place, down to the pigeon-house in the brewery-yard, which had been blown crooked on its pole by some high wind, and would have made the pigeons think themselves at sea, if there had been any pigeons there to be rocked by it. But there were no pigeons in the dove-cot, no horses in the stable, no pigs in the sty, no malt in the storehouse, no smells of grains and beer in the copper or the vat. All the uses and scents of the brewery might have evaporated with its last reek of smoke. In a by-yard, there was a wilderness of empty casks, which had a certain sour remembrance of better days lingering about them; but it was too sour to be accepted as a sample of the beer that was gone, – and in this respect I remember those recluses as being like most others.

Behind the furthest end of the brewery, was a rank garden with an old wall; not so high but that I could struggle up and hold on long enough to look over it, and see that the rank garden was the garden of the house, and that it was overgrown with tangled weeds, but that there was a track upon the green and yellow paths, as if some one sometimes walked there, and that Estella was walking away from me even then. But she seemed to be everywhere. For when I yielded to the temptation presented by the casks, and began to walk on them, I saw her walking on them at the end of the yard of casks. She had her back towards me, and held her pretty brown hair spread out in her two hands, and never looked round, and passed out of my view directly. So, in the brewery itself, – by which I mean the large paved lofty place in which they used to make the beer, and where the brewing utensils still were. When I first went into it, and, rather oppressed by its gloom, stood near the door looking about me, I saw her pass among the extinguished fires, and ascend some light iron stairs, and go out by a gallery high overhead, as if she were going out into the sky.

Great Expectations, **Charles Dickens, 1861**

Of the three large commercial companies [in Burton upon Trent] only Marston's – which started brewing in 1834 and moved to its present site, the Albion Brewery in 1898 – stays true to the traditional system of brewing in the town, a system rooted in the union room. The union method went hand in hand with the growth of pale ale brewing in the 19th century. The new style of beer was marketed on its clarity and natural sparkle. As glass replaced pewter as drinking vessels in pubs, drinkers became more aware of the murkiness of dark beers and the pleasing transluscent quality of pale ale. But producing clear beer was not easy. Yeast was in suspension in the fermenting wort. It could be skimmed from the top of the vessel but it was impossible to remove it entirely, with the result that the finished beer could be cloudy at a time when pub-goers, to use modern marketing language, were 'drinking with their eyes'. The problem was solved with the unions. Although the method is indissolubly linked with Burton upon Trent, it was invented by the Liverpool brewer Peter Walker, who briefly had a brewery in Burton at the height of the pale ale revolution. Walker simply took a medieval method of fermentation and stood it on its head. In the middle ages fermentation took place in large wooden casks. The spontaneous violence of the action of the yeast drove fermenting wort out of the open bung. Brewers collected liquid and yeast in buckets or troughs beneath the casks. They returned the liquid by hand to the casks and retained the yeast for later brews. The simple genius of Walker's method was to place troughs above the casks. The troughs retained more yeast and, because they were slightly inclined, allowed the fermenting wort to run back into the casks.

Marston's devotion to the unions is based on the belief that the yeast strain developed in the system is not only crucial to the flavour and character of its ales but would change dramatically if it were asked to work in conventional fermenters.

The union rooms at Marston's are the cathedrals of brewing. Due reverence is shown by workers and visitors, who tend to speak in hushed tones as they walk the floors and gangways of the vast rooms, where the only other sounds are the hiss of carbon dioxide and the drip, drip of foaming wort gushing from the union casks and up into the 'barm troughs' above them – barm comes from an old Norse word for yeast and is a dialect expression in Staffordshire and the North.

Fermentation at Marston's begins in open square fermenters, based in rooms above the union sets. The open vessels are unusually shallow. Head brewer Paul Bayley says that one of the many curious characteristics of yeast developed in the union system is that it will refuse point-blank to work in a conventional deep vessel. Thirty-six hours after fermentation has started, the wort is 'dropped' (run by gravity) from the shallow vessels into the union casks below.

The term union stems from the fact that the great oak casks, each one holding 144 gallons, are linked in rows by pipes and troughs – 'held in union'. A union 'set' is made up of two rows of casks, eight casks to a row, with a barm trough set above them. Each cask is cooled by water pumped through internal pipes or attemperators. As fermentation continues, carbon dioxide drives wort and yeast up swan-neck pipes built into the bung holes of each cask and which over hang the barm troughs. The wort runs back into the casks via union pipes while some of the yeast sediments in the trough. By the time fermentation has finished, nearly all the yeast has been collected in the troughs, leaving a clear beer in the casks.

The Ale Trail, **Roger Protz, 1995**

Malt is the basic ingredient for the manufacture of beer, and for hundreds of years the maltster has made the best malt from the best barley. There are several reasons why barley is the most suitable cereal. Firstly it has always been considered that malted barley produces the most desirable flavours. Barley has a husk which maize and wheat do not have, and this husk forms a filter bed when the malt is mashed in the brewery, which is an essential part of the brewing process. Also barley is the most readily available cereal in the UK. With wheat malt the germ breaks easily, allowing undesirable moulds to flourish. But for one reason or another, cereals other than barley are in use and certainly have some influence – not always bad – on the palate of the beer. Some wheat beers in Germany are labelled as such and have a quite different palate from barley beers.

The malting process itself is a very skilful operation and consists of a controlled germination of the barley which is finally stopped by heat. The hard barley is transformed into tender malt with a pleasant biscuit flavour, but the malted grain has the same outward appearance as the original barley. The insoluble starch in the barley corn is converted during germination into soluble starch which the brewers can easily convert into a fermentable sugar solution. Finally the malt is 'screened' to remove rootlets which form during germination.

Traditional maltings are very conspicuous buildings, and it is in these that the maltster soaked the barley in water for about sixty hours and then spread the grains on the malting floor in a thick and even layer to await germination. The art of the maltster was to control the temperature of the growing malt with the greatest care by turning and spreading the barley with various shovels and forks. The maltster often walked barefoot on the malting floors to avoid damage to the growing grains which could then become mouldy. The process of flooring lasted about ten days after which the temperature was allowed to rise to about 68 degrees F (20 degrees C) to stop further growth. The 'green' malt was then loaded on to a kiln where it was dried. The purpose of this was stop further growth and to cure the malt which gave it its characteristic biscuit flavour. This was a very critical operation before thermometers came to the aid of the maltster, because the temperature had to be high enough to cure the malt but not too high, otherwise the enzymes in the embryo would be destroyed (they would be necessary in the brewing process to come, for converting the starch into sugar). This is the basic malting process and it is the same today except that modern methods have become very scientific and mechanised.

The Beer Drinker's Companion, **Frank Baillie, 1973**

The Beer Drinker's Companion *appeared just two years after CAMRA was founded and became a seminal text. It was the first book to give detailed information about beer, ingredients and brewing at a time when brewers were secretive and would not even declare the strengths of their beers.*

Warren's Malthouse was enclosed by an old wall inwrapped with ivy, and though not much of the exterior was visible at this hour, the character and purposes of the building were clearly enough shown by its outline upon the sky. From the walls an overhanging thatched roof sloped up to a point in the centre, upon which rose a small wooden lantern, fitted with louvre-boards on all the four sides, and from these openings a mist was dimly perceived to be escaping into the night air. There was no window in front; but a square hole in the door was glazed with a single pane, through which red, comfortable rays now stretched out upon the ivied wall in front. Voices were to be heard inside. Oak's hand skimmed the surface of the door with fingers extended to an Elymasthe-Sorcerer pattern, till he found a leathern strap, which he pulled. This lifted a wooden latch, and the door swung open. The room inside was lighted only by the ruddy glow from the kiln mouth, which shone over the floor with the streaming horizontality of the setting sun, and threw upwards the shadows of all facial irregularities in those assembled around. The stone-flag floor was worn into a path from the doorway to the kiln, and into undulations everywhere. A curved settle of unplaned oak stretched along one side, and in a remote corner was a small bed and bedstead, the owner and frequent occupier of which was the maltster. This aged man was now sitting opposite the fire, his frosty white hair and beard overgrowing his gnarled figure like the grey moss and lichen upon a leafless apple-tree. He wore breeches and the laced-up shoes called ankle-jacks; he kept his eyes fixed upon the fire. Gabriel's nose was greeted by an atmosphere laden with the sweet smell of new malt.

Far from the Madding Crowd, **Thomas Hardy, 1874**

Long before I'd heard of CAMRA I'd virtually given up drinking in pubs in London. All you could get was Watney's Red Barrel and Double Diamond. It was the late Sixties and I'd grown up drinking Friary Meux in Guildford and Morrells in Oxford. I didn't know anything about how beer was made or anything about the politics of the big breweries. I just knew that the liquid stuff that came out of a small tap instead of a handpump was gassy and didn't have a good taste.

It was many years later that I began hearing about Real Ale! What CAMRA did for me was to put the whole thing in perspective. It taught me about beer and I shall always be grateful for that education. In 1977 Richard Boston (who was then famous as the *Guardian*'s Beer Correspondent), Martin Griffiths and I set up a micro-brewery in Hereford. We reckoned it was the first one of the new wave of micro-breweries. CAMRA very kindly let us run a story about it and helped us to recruit a brewer, Peter Austin, who had been the head brewer at Hull Brewery.

CAMRA helped get us publicity, and other would-be brewers came and learnt from our mistakes. David Bruce, for one, who realised that we spent a lot of time filling barrels and transporting them to pubs, said that it would be better to brew and sell on the same spot. That was the birth of the Firkin chain. It was wonderful to see how the micro-breweries have flourished since our first attempt – there are around 450 of them now.

Beer, for me, is something I like drinking. It's a litmus test of civilisation. If the society is making good beer, then it's a healthy society. If that sounds preposterous, look at it like this. Beer – real beer – is something that you can only make if you love it. If you want to make money, then you won't make beer – not real beer – you'll end up making something that looks like beer but that isn't really beer at all. By the time you've filtered it to take out the yeast sediment, sterilised it, and put it under the pressure of CO_2, you'll end up with an inert, lifeless corpse of a drink, dolled up with gas to pass itself off as living. Making real ale demands dedication and affection for the product. It's a real and alive thing. That's what makes it difficult to keep and that's what makes it worth looking for. A society that can still produce real beer has still preserved some values that are not based on greed and profit.

'My Love Affair with Beer', Terry Jones, *Good Beer Guide,* **2002**

Terry Jones is a writer and film producer and one of the founders of Monty Python. The brewery he helped set up was Penrhos on the Hereford/Welsh border. For the Python re-union shows in London in 2015 he ordered supplies of Python IPA from the Little Valley Brewery in Yorkshire.

> Cecily Parsley lived in a pen,
> And brewed good ale for gentlemen;
>
> Gentlemen came every day,
> Till Cecily Parsley ran away.
>
> *Cecily Parsley's Nursery Rhymes,*
> **Beatrix Potter, 1922**

One of the hallmarks of Britain's beer revolution has to be the explosion of new beer styles suddenly available to beer-lovers. Golden ales were the first, but now brewers are throwing away the rulebook and style guidelines and experimenting with new flavour combinations. Black IPA is arguably the most contentious new beer style to have emerged in recent years. For a start there's the issue of the name. Critics (Roger Protz among them) ask how can you have an India Pale Ale that is also black? Other names have been suggested, but none has gained traction, so black IPA still remains on the bar top: a beer with the aromatic character of an IPA but the colour of the middle of the night.

The passion surrounding this highly drinkable beer style is indicative of the way people feel about beer, especially during the current boom of British artisanal brewing. There's another element to the debate about black IPA, though: this is that many modern brewers, taking their cues from across the Atlantic, are getting hold of beer styles and mutating or innovating them...

It's not only in IPA that innovation can be seen. Other beer styles – whether British or from elsewhere – have been tinkered with. Stouts and porters have had fruit or spices added to them. Over at Burning Sky in Sussex brewer Mark Tranter had a dark beer slumbering away within a wine barrel. 'I used a stout recipe but added our house *Brettanomyces* and *Lacto* to it,' he said, 'then it spent eight months in a French oak barrel that had previously held Chianti. Our *Brett* is quite gentle so the result was a beer with gentle roast notes alongside equally gentle barnyard and red wine characteristics. I believe in pushing the boundaries of beer, but sensibly.' When we spoke he was getting ready to brew a porter, which would use local hops and be aged in the same Chianti barrel as the previous beer, again with added *Brettanomyces*.

Britain's Beer Revolution, Adrian Tierney-Jones, 2014

Brettanomyces – *Brett for short – is a 'wild' as opposed to cultured yeast strain. It is used primarily to make Belgian lambic beers where yeasts in the atmosphere are encouraged to enter the brewery and start fermentation.*

In July 2010, a small brewery in the Scottish fishing port of Fraserburgh produced what was, at the time, the world's strongest beer. Named after the Francis Fukuyama book that declared liberal capitalist democracy the peak of human political evolution, The End of History was, according to its makers, in a sense, the end of beer.

At 55% alcohol-by-volume, the brew, a 'blond Belgian ale infused with Scottish Highland nettles and fresh juniper berries', was stronger than most whiskies, vodkas and gins. It sold in a limited run of 11 bottles, each artfully stuffed inside a deceased wild animal – seven stoats, four grey squirrels – costing between £500 and £700.

One of the brewery's two founders, James Watt, pronounced the drink 'an audacious blend of eccentricity, artistry and rebellion'. In their 'striking packaging', Watt said, the bottles were 'disrupting conventions and breaking taboos – just like the beer they hold within them'. Not everyone agreed. Although the stoats and squirrels in question had died of natural causes, the charity Advocates for Animals denounced 'perverse' and 'out-of-date shock tactics' that 'exploited and degraded animals'. Alcohol action groups deplored a 'cheap marketing stunt' that was deliberately promoting excess in a nation with a well-known drink problem.

Watt and Martin Dickie, who met at school and launched their upstart brewery in 2007, both aged 24, stood by their creation, which they had made in a local ice-cream factory by repeatedly chilling the brew and skimming off the ice to separate the water and concentrate the alcohol (which freezes at a lower temperature).

The End of History would clearly only ever be consumed in 'very small servings,' Watt said. The brewery was simply showing people that beer could be something more than Stella, Carling or Tennent's – that it could, in fact, be 'something they had never imagined' (such as stronger than whisky). The company, he pointed out, also made a highly-flavoured beer with a very low alcohol content.

Besides, Watt could think of no better way to celebrate the lives of 11 fine specimens of dead British wildlife than ensuring that rather than being left to rot, their perfectly preserved corpses, stuffed by a master taxidermist from Doncaster, would be 'forever cherished' by the buyers of what was without doubt the most expensive beer in the world.

The End of History happened six years ago. It was a gimmick, a stunt, obviously. It also, sort of, was not. The company that pulled it, BrewDog, is a serial offender: it has, among other antics, driven a tank down Camden High Street; named a beer after the heroin-and-cocaine cocktail that killed River Phoenix and John Belushi; projected naked images of its two founders onto the Houses of Parliament; brewed beer at the bottom of the Atlantic Ocean; dropped stuffed cats from a helicopter onto the City of London; employed a dwarf to petition parliament for the introduction of a two-thirds pint glass; and released, for the royal wedding of 2011, a beer containing so-called natural aphrodisiacs such as 'herbal Viagra, chocolate and horny goat weed, which it called Royal Virility Performance.

BrewDog has described itself as a 'post-punk, apocalyptic, motherfucker of a craft brewery' and urged its customers to 'ride toward anarchy'. Its slogans include 'In hops we trust,' 'This is the revolution – so help me Dog,' and 'Changing the world, one glass at a time.' It has a document that it calls its charter, which contains phrases such as: 'We bleed craft beer,' 'We blow shit up,' and 'Without us, we are nothing. We are BrewDog.'

> **'The aggressive, outrageous, infuriating**
> **(and ingenious) rise of BrewDog', Jon Henley,**
> ***The Guardian,* 2016**

GREAT PUBS

> A good local pub has much in common
> with a church, except that a pub is warmer,
> and there's more conversation.
>
> **William Blake**

There's no such beast as 'the English pub', let alone 'the British pub'. In Scotland, for example, pubs are often called 'drinking shops' and north of Edinburgh and Glasgow beer is consumed in bars and hotels. The pub doesn't travel well and most foreign interpretations, despite being dubbed the Pig & Whistle or the Dog & Duck, bear little resemblance to the real thing.

The lack of a common style or theme for the pub is due to the fact that it constantly evolves. The first 'public houses' were just the homes of people that happened to brew the best ale in the town or village. As towns and cities grew, alehouses, inns and taverns developed to accommodate both drinkers and travellers. In the 18th and 19th centuries, coaching inns sprang up along such major routes as the Great North Road and they in turn were replaced by pubs built alongside stations when the age of steam replaced horse-drawn conveyances.

Pubs are a kaleidoscope of styles and history. Modern versions stand in close proximity to ancient inns. We can still stare agape at such historic inns as Ye Trip to Jerusalem in Nottingham and Ye Olde Fighting Cocks in St Albans and then move on a friendly local built in the 20th century. There are ornate gin palaces, pubs that celebrate both Art Nouveau and Art Deco, and the risible yet oddly pleasurable 'Brewers' Tudor' piles with their nailed-on beams and serving wenches.

Today there are the extravaganzas of Wetherspoon outlets in former banks, cinemas and even army recruitment offices.

Sadly, the chain no longer includes the Moon Under Water in Barnet, North London, that celebrated Orwell's celebrated essay about a pub so wonderful it couldn't actually exist: Wetherspoon seems to have proved him right.

In the modern age, with fast-food outlets and coffee shops proliferating on every high street, and grossly unfair competition from heavily-discounted supermarket beer, pubs are suffering. They are closing at the rate of 29 a week and the total number of pubs in the country has fallen from 70,000 in the 1970s to less than 50,000 today. But the pub is reinventing itself. Pop-up or micropubs now number 250 and are based in such unlikely places as former butcher's shop, pharmacies and bookmaker's. They are tiny, often with room for twenty people standing, but what they may lack in creature comforts is balanced by good, cheap beer.

'Underneath the Arches' would seem to the theme song for other new style pubs. Manchester in particular has a plethora of modern pubs built under rail tracks, such as the Knott opposite Deansgate station, with trains and the Metro rumbling overhead. The Piccadilly Tap, in the arcade of shops leading to Manchester's main train station, not only offers a range of beers but, sells them, sensibly, in takeaway containers for commuters.

Pubs are so vital to communities that they figure centrally in such famous TV 'soaps' as EastEnders and Coronation Street. Would the Queen Vic and the Rovers Return have such dramatic appeal if they were called Bill's Bar or Bab's Bar? Pub names are part of their history, a fact not always appreciated when they are recreated abroad. A so-called English pub near Dallas in Texas was named the Queen's Head but the owner made the cardinal error of using an image of Elizabeth II on the sign, failing to understand that English pubs only celebrate a monarch when he or she has died.

My favourite public-house, the Moon Under Water, is only two minutes from a bus stop, but is on a side-street, and drunks and rowdies never seem to find their way there, even on Saturday nights. Its clientele, though fairly large, consists mostly of 'regulars' who occupy the same chair every evening and go there for conversation as much as for the beer.

If you are asked why you favour a particular public-house, it would seem natural to put the beer first, but the thing that appeals to me about the Moon Under Water is what people call its 'atmosphere'.

To begin with, its whole architecture and fittings are uncompromisingly Victorian. It has no glass-topped tables or other modern miseries, and, on the other hand, no sham roof-beams, ingle-nooks or plastic panels masquerading as oak. The grained woodwork, the ornamental mirrors behind the bar, the cast-iron fireplaces, the florid ceiling stained dark yellow by tobacco-smoke, the stuffed bull's head over the mantelpiece – everything has the solid, comfortable ugliness of the nineteenth century.

In winter there is generally a good fire burning in at least two of the bars, and the Victorian lay-out of the place gives one plenty of elbow-room. There are a public bar, a saloon bar, a ladies' bar, a bottle-and-jug for those who are too bashful to buy their supper beer publicly, and, upstairs, a dining-room.

Games are only played in the public, so that in the other bars you can walk about without constantly ducking to avoid flying darts.

In the Moon Under Water it is always quiet enough to talk. The house possesses neither a radio nor a piano, and even on Christmas Eve and such occasions the singing that happens is of a decorous kind.

The barmaids know most of their customers by name, and take a personal interest in everyone. They are all middle-aged women – two of them have their hair dyed in quite surprising shades – and they call everyone 'dear,' irrespective of age or sex. ('Dear,' not 'Ducky': pubs where the barmaid calls you 'ducky' always have a disagreeable raffish atmosphere.)

Unlike most pubs, the Moon Under Water sells tobacco as well as cigarettes, and it also sells aspirins and stamps, and is obliging about letting you use the telephone.

You cannot get dinner at the Moon Under Water, but there is always the snack counter where you can get liver-sausage sandwiches, mussels (a speciality of the house), cheese, pickles and those large biscuits with caraway seeds in them which only seem to exist in public-houses.

Upstairs, six days a week, you can get a good, solid lunch – for example, a cut off the joint, two vegetables and boiled jam roll – for about three shillings.

The special pleasure of this lunch is that you can have draught stout with it. I doubt whether as many as 10 per cent of London pubs serve draught stout, but the Moon Under Water is one of them. It is a soft, creamy sort of stout, and it goes better in a pewter pot.

They are particular about their drinking vessels at the Moon Under Water, and never, for example, make the mistake of serving a pint of beer in a handleless glass. Apart from glass and pewter mugs, they have some of those pleasant strawberry-pink china ones which are now seldom seen in London. China mugs went out about 30 years ago, because most people like their drink to be transparent, but in my opinion beer tastes better out of china.

The great surprise of the Moon Under Water is its garden. You go through a narrow passage leading out of the saloon, and find yourself in a fairly large garden with plane trees, under which there are little green tables with iron chairs round them. Up at one end of the garden there are swings and a chute for the children.

On summer evenings there are family parties, and you sit under the plane trees having beer or draught cider to the tune of delighted squeals from children going down the chute. The prams with the younger children are parked near the gate.

Many as are the virtues of the Moon Under Water, I think that the garden is its best feature, because it allows whole families to go there instead of Mum having to stay at home and mind the baby while Dad goes out alone.

And though, strictly speaking, they are only allowed in the garden, the children tend to seep into the pub and even to fetch drinks for their parents. This, I believe, is against the law, but it is a law that deserves to be broken, for it is the puritanical nonsense of excluding children – and therefore, to some extent, women – from pubs that has turned these places into mere boozing-shops instead of the family gathering-places that they ought to be.

The Moon Under Water is my ideal of what a pub should be – at any rate, in the London area. (The qualities one expects of a country pub are slightly different.)

But now is the time to reveal something which the discerning and disillusioned reader will probably have guessed already. There is no such place as the Moon Under Water.

That is to say, there may well be a pub of that name, but I don't know of it, nor do I know any pub with just that combination of qualities.

I know pubs where the beer is good but you can't get meals, others where you can get meals but which are noisy and crowded, and others which are quiet but where the beer is generally sour. As for gardens, offhand I can only think of three London pubs that possess them.

But, to be fair, I do know of a few pubs that almost come up to the Moon Under Water. I have mentioned above ten qualities that the perfect pub should have and I know one pub that has eight of them. Even there, however, there is no draught stout, and no china mugs.

And if anyone knows of a pub that has draught stout, open fires, cheap meals, a garden, motherly barmaids and no radio, I should be glad to hear of it, even though its name were something as prosaic as the Red Lion or the Railway Arms.

'The Moon Under Water', George Orwell, *Evening Standard* 1946

If you stop at Sonning, put up at the Bull, behind the church. It is a veritable picture of an old country inn, with green, square courtyard in front, where, on seats beneath the trees, the old men group of an evening to drink their ale and gossip over village politics; with low, quaint rooms and latticed windows, and awkward stairs and winding passages.

Three Men in a Boat, Jerome K Jerome, 1889

Those entering the Saloon Bar of The Midnight Bell from the street came through a large door with a fancifully frosted glass pane, a handle like a dumb-bell, a brass inscription '*Saloon Bar and Lounge.*' and a brass adjuration to Push. Anyone temperamentally so wilful, crass, or incredulous as to ignore this friendly admonition was instantly snubbed, for this door actually would only succumb to Pushing. Nevertheless hundreds of temperamental people nightly argued with this door and got the worst of it.

Given proper treatment, however, it swung back in the most accomplished way, and announced you to the Saloon Bar with a most welcoming creak. The Saloon Bar was narrow and about thirty feet in length. On your right was the bar itself, in all its bottly glitter, and on your left was a row of tables set against a comfortable and continuous leather seat which went the whole length of the bar. At the far end the Saloon Bar opened out into the Saloon Lounge. This was a large, square room, filled with a dozen or so small, round, copper-covered tables. Around each were three or four white wicker armchairs, and on each table there lay a large stone ash-tray supplied by a Whisky firm. The walls were lined with a series of prints depicting moustached cavalrymen in a variety of brilliant uniforms; there was a fireplace with a well-provided fire; the floor was of chessboard oil-cloth, broken by an occasional mat, and the whole atmosphere was spotless, tidy, bright, and a little chilly. This was no scene for the brawler, but rather for the principled and restrained drinker, with his wife. In here and in the Saloon Bar 'The Midnight Bell' did most of its business – the other two bars (the Public and the Private) being dreary, seatless, bareboarded structures wherein drunkenness was dispensed in coarser tumblers and at a cheaper rate to a mostly collarless and frankly downtrodden stratum of society. The Public Bar could nevertheless be glimpsed by a customer in the Saloon Bar, and as the evening wore on it provided the latter with an acoustic background of deep mumbling and excited talk without which its whole atmosphere would have been lost – without which, indeed, the nightly drama of the Saloon Bar would have been rather like a cinematograph without music...

The Midnight Bell, **Patrick Hamilton, 1929**

Gordon moved back to the saloon bar. The window was frosted, and also steamy from the heat inside. Still, there were chinks where you could see through. He peeped in. Yes, Flaxman was there.

The saloon bar was crowded. Like all rooms seen from the outside, it looked ineffably cosy. The fire that blazed in the grate danced, mirrored, in the brass spittoons. Gordon thought he could almost smell the beer through the glass. Flaxman was propping up the bar with two fish-faced pals who looked like insurance-touts of the better type. One elbow on the bar, his foot on the rail, a beer-streaked glass in the other hand, he was swapping backchat with the blonde cutie barmaid. She was standing on a chair behind the bar, ranging the bottled beer and talking saucily over her shoulder. You couldn't hear what they were saying, but you could guess. Flaxman let fall some memorable witticism. The fish-faced men bellowed with obscene laughter. And the blonde cutie, tittering down at him, half shocked and half delighted, wriggled her neat little bum.

Gordon's heart sickened. To be in there, just to be in there! In the warmth and light, with people to talk to, with beer and cigarettes and a girl to flirt with! After all, why not go in? You could borrow a bob off Flaxman. Flaxman would lend it to you all right. He pictured Flaxman's careless assent – 'What ho, chappie! How's life? What? A bob? Sure! Take two. Catch, chappie!' – and the florin flicked along the beer-wet bar. Flaxman was a decent sort, in his way.

Gordon put his hand against the swing door. He even pushed it open a few inches. The warm fog of smoke and beer slipped through the crack. A familiar, reviving smell; nevertheless as he smelled it his nerve failed him. No! Impossible to go in. He turned away. He couldn't go shoving in that saloon bar with only fourpence halfpenny in his pocket. Never let other people buy your drinks for you! The first commandment of the moneyless. He made off, down the dark pavement.

Keep the Aspidistra Flying, George Orwell, 1936

One of the principal attractions of the inn was our cavalier attitude towards closing time. In those days, pub licensing hours were still very restricted – the official hours were 11 to 3 and 5.30 to 10.30 – but the Inn at the Top was a place where the normal rules didn't apply – at least as long as the police weren't watching. If time did not exactly stand still, it never seemed to be called and, just like the Windmill Theatre in the Second World War, our proudest boast was: 'We never closed'.

The police were under orders to make regular after hours inspections of all the pubs in their area, but the police station was twenty miles away, along some of the most narrow and twisting roads in the country, without a single street light, white line or cats' eye to guide a motorist after dark. They were understandably reluctant to make that journey any more often than they had to, and as a result the Inn at the Top became the only pub in the country to be raided by prior appointment. Every couple of months, the phone would ring and an anonymous, but unmistakably policeman-like voice would say 'Mr Hanson? Mr Neil Hanson? A word to the wise, sir. The police will be paying you a visit at eleven o'clock tonight.' He didn't add 'Evening all,' or 'Mind how you go', but not even the dimmest bulb in the box could have been in any doubt about his occupation.

The police duly appeared at 11 that night but found the door locked and the pub in darkness... albeit with a surprisingly large number of cars still in the car-park. Having tried the door and peered through the windows, honour was satisfied and they disappeared back down the hill, whereupon the lights came back on, and a dozen farmers who'd been waiting out the raid in darkness and silence, standing in the kitchen clutching their pint pots, were ushered back through to the bar and normal service was resumed.

Nonetheless, we took the precaution of applying to the magistrates for a two-hour extension on the night of the annual sheep show – the biggest night of the pub's year but to my horror, when I attended the hearing, the chairman of the magistrates told me that he was turning us down. However after a few beats of silence, he gave the ghost of a wink and added: 'Since I understand that the pub is already open 24 hours a day, I can't for the life of me see how it would be physically possible to extend the drinking hours any further.'

The Inn at the Top, Neil Hanson, 2013

The Tan Hill Inn, the highest in England, is in Swaledale, North Yorkshire.

The bar of the Six Jolly Fellowship-Porters was a bar to soften the human breast. The available space in it was not much larger than a hackney-coach; but no one could have wished the bar bigger, that space was so girt in by corpulent little casks, and by cordial-bottles radiant with fictitious grapes in bunches, and by lemons in nets, and by biscuits in baskets, and by the polite beer-pulls that made low bows when customers were served with beer, and by the cheese in a snug corner, and by the landlady's own small table in a snugger corner near the fire, with the cloth everlastingly laid. This haven was divided from the rough world by a glass partition and a half-door, with a leaden sill upon it for the convenience of resting your liquor; but, over this half-door the bar's snugness so gushed forth, that, albeit customers drank there standing, in a dark and draughty passage where they were shouldered by other customers passing in and out, they always appeared to drink under an enchanting delusion that they were in the bar itself.

Our Mutual Friend, **Charles Dickens, 1865**

Round Clifton Hampden, itself a wonderfully pretty village, old-fashioned, peaceful, and dainty with flowers, the river scenery is rich and beautiful. If you stay the night on land at Clifton, you cannot do better than put up at the 'Barley Mow.' It is, without exception, I should say, the quaintest, most old-world inn up the river. It stands on the right of the bridge, quite away from the village. Its low-pitched gables and thatched roof and latticed windows give it quite a story-book appearance, while inside it is even still more once-upon-a-timeyfied.

It would not be a good place for the heroine of a modern novel to stay at. The heroine of a modern novel is always 'divinely tall,' and she is ever 'drawing herself up to her full height.' At the 'Barley Mow' she would bump her head against the ceiling each time she did this.

It would also be a bad house for a drunken man to put up at. There are too many surprises in the way of unexpected steps down into this room and up into that; and as for getting upstairs to his bedroom, or ever finding his bed when he got up, either operation would be an utter impossibility to him.

Three Men in a Boat, Jerome K Jerome, **1889**

The pub, reduced to its lowest terms, is a house where during certain hours everyone is free to buy and drink a glass of beer. It is the only kind of public building used by large numbers of ordinary people where their thoughts and actions are not being in some way arranged for them; in the other kinds of public buildings they are the audiences, watchers of political, religious, dramatic, cinematic, instructional or athletic spectacles. But within the four walls of the pub, once a man has bought or been bought his glass of beer, he has entered an environment in which he is participator rather than spectator.

The Pub and The People: a Worktown Study,
Mass Observation, 1943

Mass Observation, founded in 1937, recorded everyday social life through a panel of volunteer observers. Its work ended in the mid-1960s but it was revived in 1981. Its archives are held at the University of Sussex.

LANDLORDS AND LANDLADIES

> **BET LYNCH** *I was pulling pints before I was legally old enough to drink 'em. And I've been doing it ever since. I've given meself body and soul to the public house trade. There's not a lot I don't know about pubs. And even less I don't know about customers.*
>
> Coronation Street, 1984

From the earliest times, ale and beer have been served by people who at first brewed on their own premises or, in more recent times, made available the products of commercial brewers. It wasn't until the Industrial Revolution of the late 18th and 19th centuries that brewing in inns and pubs went out of fashion as commercial brewers started to build 'tied estates'. The earliest inns in the Anglo-Saxon and medieval periods grew out of humble dwellings where the ale produced in them was considered to be superior to that of its neighbours'. An ale-stake or ale-pole was erected and decorated with a green bush to announce that a fresh batch of ale was ready for consumption: pubs today called the Bush recall those times.

Brewing was usually conducted by the woman of the house, who made bread and ale from the same ingredients. Women brewers were known as brewsters or ale-wives and their central role in dispensing good beer survives today in the form of landladies such as Bet Lynch in Coronation Street. *Landladies such as Bet could even be considered a descendant of famous London tavern keeper, Mistress Quickly, who had to keep the likes of Sir John Falstaff and his cronies in good order. Barmaids may have a more subsidiary role but they are equally important to the running of a good pub and their ability to spot a regular and offer 'a pint of the usual' is legendary. Some of the quotations here about barmaids would not be considered politically correct today but they are of their time and were written with affection.*

As commercial brewing developed following the collapse of feudalism and the grip of the church, men began to play a more central role in both making and dispensing beer. An old English folk song stresses their vital role: 'Come landlord fill the flowing bowl until it doth run over' and the 'the guv'nor's' rosy-cheeked contribution to the joys of the pub is commemorated in the works of Dickens and many other writers, though Dickens was also aware of the matriarchal power of landladies, as seen in his portrait of the lady of the house in the Six Jolly Fellowship Porters.

Finally, however, they had found courage to enter, and duly met Stannidge the landlord; a silent man, who drew and carried frothing measures to this room and to that, shoulder to shoulder with his waiting-maids – a stately slowness, however, entering into his ministrations by contrast with theirs, as became one whose service was somewhat optional. It would have been altogether optional but for the orders of the landlady, a person who sat in the bar, corporeally motionless, but with a flitting eye and quick ear, with which she observed and heard through the open door and hatchway the pressing needs of customers whom her husband overlooked though close at hand.

The Mayor of Casterbridge, **Thomas Hardy, 1886**

Miss Potterson, sole proprietor and manager of the Fellowship Porters, reigned supreme on her throne, the Bar, and a man must have drunk himself mad drunk indeed if he thought he could contest a point with her... 'Now, you mind, you Riderhood,' said Miss Abbey Potterson, with emphatic forefinger over the half-door, 'the Fellowship don't want you at all and would rather by far have your room than your company; but if you were as welcome here as you are not, you shouldn't even then have another drop of drink here this night, after this present pint of beer. So make the most of it'.

Our Mutual Friend, **Charles Dickens, 1865**

The Six Jolly Fellowship Porters was based on the Grapes in Narrow Street, Limehouse, London E14. It is owned today by Sir Ian McKellen, Evgeny Lebedev and Sean Mathias.

In a quarter of an hour we were in Bloomsbury at the Alpha Inn, which is a small public-house at the corner of one of the streets which runs down into Holborn. Holmes pushed open the door of the private bar, and ordered two glasses of beer from the ruddy-faced, white-aproned landlord.

The Adventure of the Blue Carbuncle,
Arthur Conan Doyle, 1892

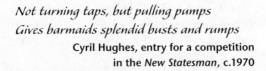

Not turning taps, but pulling pumps
Gives barmaids splendid busts and rumps
Cyril Hughes, entry for a competition
in the *New Statesman*, c.1970

FORD PREFECT:	Six pints of bitter, and quickly please, the world's about to end.
BARMAN:	Oh yes, sir? Nice weather for it. Going to watch the match this afternoon?
FORD PREFECT:	No, no point.
BARMAN:	Foregone conclusion you reckon sir. Arsenal without a chance?
FORD PREFECT:	No it's just that the world's going to end.
BARMAN:	Ah yes you said. Lucky escape for Arsenal if it did.

The Hitch Hikers Guide to the Galaxy, Douglas Adams, 1978

Half an hour afterwards Dick emerged from the inn, and if Fancy's lips had been real cherries probably Dick's would have appeared deeply stained. When the newly betrothed young man returned to the inn yard, the jovial publican smited him playfully under the fifth rib, and said in broad Dorset: 'This will never do, upon my life, Master Dewy! Calling for tay and for a feymel passenger, and then going in and sitting down and having some too, and biding such a fine long time!'

Under the Greenwood Tree, Thomas Hardy, 1929

The inn in Hardy's novel is the Ship Inn at Upwey.

BONIFACE:	This way, this way, sir.
AIMWELL:	You're my landlord, I suppose?
BONIFACE:	Yes, sir, I'm old Will Boniface; pretty well known upon this road, so the saying is.
AIMWELL:	Oh, Boniface, your servant.
BONIFACE:	Oh, sir, what wilt your honour please to drink, as the saying is?
AIMWELL:	I have heard your town of Lichfield much famed for ales; I think I'll taste that.
BONIFACE:	Sir, I have now in my cellar ten tun of the best ale in Staffordshire: 'tis smooth as oil, sweet as milk, clear as amber, and strong as brandy, and will be just fourteen years old the fifth day of next March, old style.
AIMWELL:	You're very exact, I find, in the age of your ale.
BONIFACE:	As punctual, sir, as I am in the age of my children. I'll show you such ale. Here, tapster, broach number 1706, as the saying is. Sir, you shall taste my 'anno domini'. I have lived in Lichfield, man and boy, above eight-and-fifty years, and I believe I have not consumed eight-and-fifty ounces of meat.
AIMWELL:	At a meal, you mean, if one may guess by your bulk?
BONIFACE:	Not in my life, sir; I have fed purely upon ale. I have ate my ale, drank my ale, and I always sleep upon my ale.

(ENTER TAPSTER WITH A TANKARD)

Now, sir, you shall see...Your worship's health. (DRINKS). Ha! delicious, delicious: fancy it Burgundy, only fancy it – and 'tis worth ten shillings a quart.

AIMWELL:	(DRINKS). 'Tis confounded strong.
BONIFACE:	Strong! It must be so, or how would we be strong that drinks it?
AIMWELL:	And have you lived so long upon this ale, landlord?
BONIFACE:	Eight-and-fifty years, upon my credit, sir; but it killed my wife, poor woman, as the saying is.
AIMWELL:	How came that to pass?
BONIFACE:	I don't know how, sir; she would not let the ale take its natural course, sir; she was for qualifying it every now and then with a dram, as the saying is; and an honest gentleman, that came this way from Ireland, made her a present of a dozen bottles of usquebaugh [whisky] – but the poor woman was never well after; but, however, I was obliged to the gentleman, you know.
AIMWELL:	Why, was it the usquebaugh that killed her?
BONIFACE:	My Lady Bountiful said so. She, good lady, did what could be done: she cured her of three tympanies; but the fourth carried her off; but she's happy, and I'm contented, as the saying is.

The Beaux' Stratagem, George Farquhar, 1707

The comedy was first produced in 1707 at the Theatre Royal, Haymarket in London, now Her Majesty's Theatre.

Most barmaids are called Ruby, and they usually come from Portsmouth. It is hard to say why (our local Ruby could possibly furnish an explanation if you asked her, but this is something I do not advise, for it would mean violating a certain rule of etiquette generally observed in conversation between barmaid and customer). You can talk to a barmaid on any subject in the world – oh, yes, she's very broad-minded – except on the subject of barmaids: To acknowledge the existence of such a breed in her presence would be an impropriety of the most boorish kind. For although there is nothing discreditable in her calling, the word 'barmaid' has an unfortunate ring about it which suggests otherwise. It is a survival of the days when a pub was either a fine, flaring gin-palace or a seamy, sinful beer shop; and from the higher-minded of his ancestors the average man has inherited an ability to say 'barmaid' without sounding a faint note of contumely.

What's Yours, T E B Clarke, 1938

T E B 'Tibby' Clarke was a leading British screenwriter associated for many years with Ealing Studios. In 1952 he won an Oscar for his screenplay for The Lavender Hill Mob. *He also wrote the screenplays for* Sons & Lovers *and* The Blue Lamp.

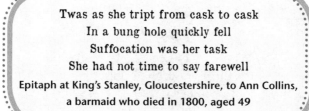

Twas as she tript from cask to cask
In a bung hole quickly fell
Suffocation was her task
She had not time to say farewell

**Epitaph at King's Stanley, Gloucestershire, to Ann Collins,
a barmaid who died in 1800, aged 49**

My pulpit is an alehouse bench,
Whereon I sit so jolly;
A smiling rosy country wench,
My saint and patron holy.
I kiss her cheek so red and sleek,
I press her ringlets wavy,
And in her willing ear I speak
A most religious Ave.

'The Devil's Wager',
William Makepeace Thackeray, 1833

And fifteen arms went round her waist.
(And then men ask Are Barmaids chaste?)

'The Everlasting Mercy', John Masefield, 1911

'Now,' he pursued, 'concerning Miss Havisham. Miss Havisham, you must know, was a spoilt child. Her mother died when she was a baby, and her father denied her nothing. Her father was a country gentleman down in your part of the world, and was a brewer. I don't know why it should be a crack thing to be a brewer; but it is indisputable that while you cannot possibly be genteel and bake, you may be as genteel as never was and brew. You see it every day.'

'Yet a gentleman may not keep a public-house; may he?' said I.

'Not on any account,' returned Herbert; 'but a public-house may keep a gentleman.'

Great Expectations, Charles Dickens, 1861

| MISTRESS QUICKLY: | If he swaggers, let him not come here: no, by my faith; I must live among my neighbours: I'll have no swaggerers: I am in good name and fame with the very best: shut the door; there come no swaggerers here: I have not lived all this while, to have swaggering now: shut the door, I pray you. |

Henry IV Part 2, **William Shakespeare, 1600**

Mistress Quickly ran the Boar Head's, Eastcheap, London.

Her lothely [loathsome] lere
Is nothynge clere,
But vgly of chere,
Droupy and drowsy,
Scuruy and lowsy;
Her face all bowsy,
Comely crynklyd,
Woundersly wrynkled,
Lyke a rost pygges eare,
Brystled with here...
Her nose somdele hoked,
And camously croked,
Neuer stoppynge;
Her skynne lose and slacke,
Grained lyke a sacke;
With a croked backe.

Skelton's poem in Middle English was based on a real-life innkeeper and brewster, Alianora Romyng, who worked in Leatherhead, Surrey, in 1525. 'Tunnyng' or tunning means running ale into tuns or casks. The quality of her ale was doubtful as she allowed chickens to roost (roust) over the mash tun:

The hennes ron in the mashfat;
For they go to roust
Streyght ouer the ale ioust,
And dong [dung], whan it commes,
In the ale tunnes.
Than Elynour taketh
The mash bolle, and shaketh
The hens donge away,
And skommeth it in a tray
Whereas the yeest is,
With her maungy fystis:
And somtyme she blennes
The donge of her hennes
And the ale together;
And sayeth, Gossyp, come hyther,
This ale shall be thycker,
And flowre [ferment] the more quicker

The Tunnyng of Elynour Rummyng, **John Skelton, 1551**

There is a noble tradition in British pubs of indomitable women licensees, who rule over their pubs with a rod of iron, reigning supreme for decades, and who are remembered with respect and, more remarkably, with great affection. One of the most indomitable of all was Lola Taplin. Her family had owned the Fleece Inn at Bretforton for over 500 years and she ran it single-handed for the last thirty years of her long life, until her death in 1977 at the age of eighty-three.

It is said that she never let customers forget that they were drinking in her family home and not just any old public house, and any who forgot their manners would be out on their ears in very quick time.

On her death, Lola Taplin left the inn, its magnificent contents and its gardens to the National Trust on condition that it continued to be run as an unspoilt country pub.

Classic Country Pubs, Neil Hanson, 1987

The Fleece in Bretforton (pronounced locally Brefferton), Worcestershire, is recognised by CAMRA's as having an interior of historic national importance. It serves beers from such local breweries as Uley and Wye Valley and has resumed making its own cider.

On the chest of a barmaid from Sale
Was tattooed all the prices of ale.
Whilst on her behind,
For the sake of the blind,
Was precisely the same, but in Braille.

Anon

This favoured tavern, sacred to the evening orgies of Mr. Lowten and his companions, was what ordinary people would designate a public-house. That the landlord was a man of a money-making turn, was sufficiently testified by the fact of a small bulk-head beneath the tap-room window, in size and shape not unlike a sedan-chair, being underlet to a mender of shoes: and that he was a being of philanthropic mind, was evident from the protection he afforded to a pieman, who vended his delicacies without fear of interruption on the very door-step. In the lower windows, which were decorated with curtains of a saffron hue, dangled two or three printed cards, bearing reference to Devonshire cyder and Dantzic spruce, while a large black board, announcing in white letters to an enlightened public that there were 500,000 barrels of double stout in the cellars of the establishment, left the mind in a state of not unpleasing doubt and uncertainty as the precise direction in the bowels of the earth, in which this mighty cavern might be supposed to extend. When we add, that the weather-beaten sign-board bore the half-obliterated semblance of a magpie intently eyeing a crooked streak of brown paint, which the neighbours had been taught from infancy to consider as the 'stump', we have said all that need to be said of the exterior of the edifice.

The Pickwick Papers, Charles Dickens, 1836

The Magpie & Stump, 18 Old Bailey, stands opposite the Central Criminal Court, better known as the Old Bailey. In the 20th century the pub was given the nickname of 'Courtroom Number One' by journalists covering trials over the road.

PUBS IN PERIL

From the towns all Inns have been driven:
from the villages most... Change your
hearts or you will lose your Inns and you
will deserve to have lost them. But when
you have lost your Inns drown your empty
selves, for you will have lost the last of
England.

'This and That and the Other', Hilaire Belloc, 1912

Inns, taverns and public houses have been under threat of
closure for as long as they have existed. When the church rose
to prominence, abbots and bishops attempted to curtail the
spread of taverns to prevent lowly monks from drinking in
them and to encourage instead the consumption of the beer
brewed on monastery premises. As the power of the church
declined, monarchs found ale houses and inns and the beers
they provided to be sitting targets for taxation to fund both
wars and the excessive life style of the royalty. The development
in the 19th century of the 'tied house' system – pubs owned
directly by brewers – led to the ruthless closure of licensed
houses, with scant regard for community interests, as recorded
vividly by Christopher Hutt in Norfolk in the 1970s. The
experience of Watneys in the 1970s has returned with a
vengeance at the turn of the 21st century. As a result of
government intervention, national brewers were forced to
divest themselves of many of their pubs. They have been
bought by new non-brewing businesses known as pub
companies or 'pubcos' for short. The bigger pubcos have

introduced a supermarket attitude to pub retailing. Publicans are charged top rates for both beer and rents and those that fail to reach the tough targets set for them find their pubs closed. The pubcos also have a keen eye on the value of property, which has seen perfectly viable pubs sold to property developers and turned into private housing.

Publicans and drinkers are fighting back. As the Good Beer Guide *reported in 2014, consumers now have a strategy that sets out to thwart the activities of the pubcos and seeks to retain pubs as vital hubs of their communities.*

There are no pubs left in Stiffkey [on the North Norfolk coast], since the last was shut down in the summer of 1971. Until the mid 1960s there were three pubs in the village which trade traditionally belonged to three separate breweries, each based in Norwich. All three breweries were swallowed up by Watneys, whose rationalisation programme arrived in Stiffkey when the Victoria, the former Steward and Patteson house, was closed in 1966...

Old Buckenham, also in Norfolk, is on the other side of the county, some forty miles from Stiffkey, but this distance has not saved the village from suffering a similar fate. Old Buckenham is three times the size of Stiffkey, with a population of almost one thousand, which as in many Norfolk villages is scattered over several square miles. There were three pubs in the village, catering for different parts of the community, until the Sun was closed... The Sun, situated at the Cake Street end of the village, is over a mile from either of the other pubs, and was an extremely popular house with its own band of dedicated locals, who resisted its closure with something more than the hopeless resignation that seems to have prevailed in Stiffkey.

Charlie Large, a retired wheelwright, has... lived in the same village all his life. Charlie is the village poet and when he first heard of plans to shut down the Sun, he dashed off a few verses and ceremonially pinned his 'Curse on the brewers' to the door of the pub:

Bad luck to all the brewers
Who close up their pubs,
May their profits dwindle
And their wives all cease to love.

May they sit around the boardroom
With their faces drawn and glum,
May they forever rue the day
When they closed Old Buckenham Sun.

This pub has been the same
For a hundred years or more,
With a good coal fire to heat it,
And pamments on the floor.

If you want a posh place
With carpets on the floor
Yes, you can have it
But the beer will cost you more.

So drink some home-made cider
And you will not give a damn
If they close all the bloody pubs
That belong to Watney Mann.

The Death of the English Pub, Christopher Hutt, 1973

Stiffkey is known as 'Stookey' to the locals and the area is famous for a type of mussel known as the Stookey Blue. The Red Lion reopened in the late 1990s. Old Buckenham now has two pubs, the Gamekeeper, previously the White Horse, and the Ox & Plough.

It was rumoured that when Mr Webster (who and whose wife had been rather the personal friends of his guests than ordinary innkeepers) left the Maid's Head [Norwich], the whole scope of the old house – the nearest approach to the typical old hostel that I ever saw – was going to be changed; that it was to be let to a big brewer, and be turned into a commercial inn, with a coloured glass bar, a billiard-room, and the rest of it; and, in fact, that the whole place was to be spoiled, and no longer the refuge for those who like peace and quiet and old surroundings.

Walter Rye

Norwich historian Walter Rye purchased the Maid's Head – said to be the oldest hotel in Britain – in 1889 to prevent it from falling into the hands of a 'big brewer'.

When you asked for a pint of bitter ten years ago it was invariably served in one of two ways: usually it would raised from the cellar by a traditional beer engine, operated by a handle on the bar counter; occasionally it would be gravity-drawn from a barrel on or behind the bar. This beer would have arrived from the brewery in wood or metal (aluminium or stainless steel) casks and would be required to settle in the cellar for a day or two before serving. It would not go flat because the fermentation process was still completing itself. The simplest description of keg beer is that it is bottled beer in draught condition. The fermentation process is halted before the beer leaves the brewery by chilling, filtering and pasteurisation. When the beer has been placed in its container, the residue of air is displaced by carbon dioxide, and the container is sealed for delivery. Inside the pub cellar, the container is attached to piping, which leads to the bar, and also to a cylinder of carbon dioxide which will keep the beer under pressure and force it to the point of delivery when the tap or button is turned or pressed in the bar. Keg beer often passes through a chiller on its way to the point of dispense.

The subtle flavour of a good pint of bitter depends on the beer being relatively still and served at the right temperature. Chilled and carbonated products can never match the unique bitterness and the variety of overall palate that are available in draught beer.

The Death of the English Pub, **Christopher Hutt, 1973**

In spite of the title, the book was as much about the threats to real draught beer as it was to the pub. Christopher Hutt was the second national chairman of CAMRA and went on to run CAMRA Real Ale Investments, a small chain of pubs.

When Julia Warren, publican at the Fox & Goose [Hebden Bridge], was forced to retire on health grounds, she was determined the pub wouldn't be sold to a national pub company. The Fox & Goose has a long history as an ale house and Julia was keen to maintain the tradition of supplying beer from local breweries.

She runs two beer festivals a year – at Whitsun and in November – and the range of regular beers includes a house ale called Margery's Tiddlywink. This commemorates the early days of the pub in the 1330s, when it was an illegal ale house, known in the local dialect as a Tiddlywink. It was run by Margery de Wyndhall.

It became a legal ale house in the 17th century and flourished in modern times, winning several awards from the local Halifax & Calderdale branch of CAMRA, including its Pub of the Year in 2006.

When Julia announced her retirement, 100 local people packed in to the pub in January 2013 to discuss how to save it. The locals immediately offered to raise £8,200 towards buying the pub. A steering group, Friends of the Fox & Goose, was set up and they sought advice from the Plunkett Foundation, which advises people on how to save such local assets as village shops. Dave Hollings of Co-operative & Mutual Solutions also came to give his advice and experience. He has helped create several co-ops, including the first-ever pub to be owned and run by locals, the Old Crown at Hesket Newmarket in Cumbria.

The major breakthrough came when Calderdale Council listed the Fox & Goose as a community asset under the new Localism Act. This gave the steering group the right to make the first bid for the pub, with six months to raise the necessary money. It turned itself into the Fox & Goose (Hebden Bridge) Ltd, a co-operative or, in legal terms, an Industrial and Provident Society.

A share offer was launched on 1 May 2013 with the aim of raising £130,000. Supporters can buy shares worth a minimum of £100 and a maximum of £20,000. The share offer was due to close at the end of July. If successful, the co-op will own the building, not the business, and it will have to re-launch the pub.

Councillor Dave Young, who chairs Fox & Goose Ltd, said when the share offer was launched: 'The co-op is no longer a dream – it's a reality and exciting opportunity. Friends of the Fox believe this is a viable proposition to save a well-loved local and retain it for the community.'

> **'Landlady passes the baton to her regulars',**
> **Roger Protz, *Good Beer Guide*, 2013**

An East London licensee battling to buy his pub says he is 'hopeful' of success after raising £60,000 in under three weeks. Jack Hunter, who runs East End boozer the Queens Head in Limehouse, said to be the inspiration for *Eastenders'* the Queen Vic, is attempting to raise over a half a million pounds to buy the pub after it was put on the market by leaseholders the Unity Welfare Foundation earlier this year. The pub is listed as an Asset of Community Value (ACV), which means the local community has six months to raise the money and make a bid.

Hunter told the *Publican's Morning Advertiser*: 'We've raised quite a considerable amount so far but we still need to raise a lot more. It's the old story – the pub is the least profitable part of the building, we've got five bedrooms here and we're two miles away from Trafalgar Square. The pub has a huge amount of heritage and I'd be heartbroken if it closed.

'However, we're not out with the begging bowl. We're offering shares and people who invest will get a return. I've seen other examples of communities rescuing dilapidated pubs and that's not the cause with us, we're a trading business.'

Hunter, who operates the pub with his partner Denise West, added that he hoped to receive further funding from the Plunkett Foundation and use his connections in the music industry to organise fundraising events at the pub.

Actor and *Lord of the Rings* star Sir Ian McKellen is among the famous faces to have visited the pub and took part in a traditional Easter celebration at the Queens Head last month.

'Battle to save pub rumoured to be inspiration for Eastenders' Queen Victoria', Emily Sutherland, ***Publican's Morning Advertiser,*** **2016**

Epilogue

Up the street, in the Sailors Arms, Sinbad Sailors, grandson of Mary Ann Sailors, draws a pint in the sunlit bar. The ship's clock in the bar says half past eleven. Half past eleven is opening time. The hands of the clock have stayed still at half past eleven for fifty years. It is always opening time in the Sailors Arms.

Under Milk Wood, **Dylan Thomas, 1954**

Index of Authors

Index of Titles

The publisher gratefully acknowledges the permission granted to reproduce the copyright material in this book.

The Oxford Companion to Beer edited by Garret Oliver (Oxford University Press, 2011)

At Home: A Short History of Private Life by Bill Bryson (Doubleday, 2010)

'From Bitter to Aromatic' by Breandán Kearney (*Belgian Beer & Food*, 2016)

Beer O'Clock, Craft, Cask and Culture by Jane Peyton (Summersdale, 2013)

So You Want to Be a Beer Expert by Jeff Evans (CAMRA Books, 2015)

Beer Naturally by Michael Hardman (Bergstrom and Boyle Books Ltd, 1976)

'Old Garbo' by Dylan Thomas. Reprinted from *Portrait of the Artist as a Young Dog* (Phoenix). Permission for reprint provided by David Higham Associates Limited.

Nineteen Eighty-Four by George Orwell (Copyright © George Orwell, 1949) Reprinted by permission of Bill Hamilton as the Literary Executor of the Estate of the Late Sonia Brownell.

Good Beer Guide 1989 (CAMRA Books, 1988)

A Sort of Life by Graham Greene (Vintage). Permission for reprint provided by David Higham Associates Limited.

Let Me Tell You About Beer by Melissa Cole (Pavilion Books, 2011)

Britain's 500 Best Pubs by Roger Protz (Carlton Books Ltd, 2002)

Classic Country Pubs by Neil Hanson (CAMRA, 1987)

At Swim-Two-Birds by Flann O'Brien (Copyright © Flann O'Brien, 1939) Reprinted by permission of A.M. Heath & Co Ltd.

Animal Farm by George Orwell (Copyright © George Orwell, 1945) Reprinted by permission of Bill Hamilton as the Literary Executor of the Estate of the Late Sonia Brownell Orwell.

The Ale Trail by Roger Protz (Eric Dobby Publishing Ltd, 1995)

The Beer Drinker's Companion by Frank Baillie (David & Charles, 1973)

Cecily Parsley's Nursery Rhymes by Beatrix Potter

Good Beer Guide 2003 (CAMRA Books, 2002)

Britain's Beer Revolution by Roger Protz and Adrian Tierney-Jones (CAMRA Books, 2014)

'The aggressive, outrageous, infuriating (and ingenious) rise of BrewDog' by Jon Henly (*The Guardian*, 2016)

'The Moon Under Water' by George Orwell (Copyright © George Orwell, 1946) Reprinted by kind permission of Bill Hamilton as the Literary Executor of the Estate of the Late Sonia Brownell.

The Midnight Bell by Patrick Hamilton (Copyright © Patrick Hamilton, 1929) Reprinted by permission of A.M. Heath & Co Ltd.

Keep the Aspidistra Flying by George Orwell (Copyright © George Orwell, 1936) Reprinted by kind permission of Bill Hamilton as the Literary Executor of the Estate of the Late Sonia Brownell.

The Inn at the Top © Neil Hanson 2013

Coronation Street (ITV plc)

The Hitch Hikers Guide to the Galaxy by Douglas Adams © 1978. Reprinted by kind permission of the Estate of Douglas Adams.

'The Everlasting Mercy' by John Masefield. Permission granted by The Society of Authors as the Literary Representative of the Estate of John Masefield

'This and That and the Other' by Hilaire Belloc. Reprinted by permission of Peters Fraser & Dunlop (www.petersfraserdunlop. com) on behalf of the Estate of Hilaire Belloc.

The Death of the English Pub by Christopher Hutt (Arrow Bks, 1973)

Good Beer Guide 2014 (CAMRA Books, 2013)

'Battle to save pub rumoured to be inspiration for Eastenders' Queen Victoria' by Emily Sutherland (*The Publican's Morning Advertiser*, 2016)

Under Milk Wood by Dylan Thomas (Phoenix). Permission for reprint provided by David Higham Associates Limited.

Books for Beer Lovers

CAMRA Books, the publishing arm of the Campaign for Real Ale,
is the leading publisher of books on beer and pubs.
Key titles include:

Good Beer Guide 2017

Editor: Roger Protz

CAMRA's *Good Beer Guide* is fully revised and updated
each year and features pubs across the United Kingdom
that serve the best real ale. In its 44th edition, this pub
guide is completely independent with listings based entirely
on nomination and evaluation by CAMRA members.

£15.99   ISBN 978-1-85249-335-6   Published September 2016

The Year in Beer: 2017 Diary

Discover a beer for every week of the year with
CAMRA's *Year in Beer 2017 Diary*. The best beers from
around the world are linked to key events and dates
through the year, with comprehensive tasting notes.
Major anniversaries, religious feasts and important
birthdays are highlighted, along with commemorations,
carnivals and some more eccentric events.

£9.99   ISBN 987-1-85249-337-0   Published September 2016

CAMRA's Beer Knowledge

Jeff Evans

A fully revised and updated collection of conversation-
starting anecdotes, useful pub facts and figures, and trivia,
CAMRA's *Beer Knowledge* is the perfect gift for any beer
lover. More than 200 entries cover the serious, the silly
and the downright bizarre from the world of beer. Inside
this pint-sized compendium you'll find everything from
the biggest brewer in the world to the beers with the daftest names.

£9.99   ISBN 978-1-85249-338-7   Published October 2016

Order these and other CAMRA books online at **www.camra.org.uk/books**,
ask at your local bookstore, or contact:
CAMRA, 230 Hatfield Road, St Albans, AL1 4LW. Telephone 01727 867201

A campaign of two halves

Campaigning for pub goers and beer drinkers

CAMRA, the Campaign for Real Ale, is the not-for-profit independent voice of real ale drinkers and pub goers. CAMRA's vision is to have quality real ale and thriving pubs in every community. We campaign tirelessly to achieve this goal, as well as lobbying government to champion drinkers' rights. As a CAMRA member you will have the opportunity to campaign to save pubs under threat of closure, for pubs to be free to serve a range of real ales at fair prices and for a long-term freeze in beer duty that will help Britain's brewing industry survive.

Enjoying real ale and pubs

CAMRA has over 175,000 members from all ages and backgrounds, brought together by a common belief in the issues that CAMRA deals with and their love of good quality British beer. From just **£24** a year* – that's less than a pint a month – you can join CAMRA and enjoy the following benefits:

- Subscription to *What's Brewing*, our monthly colour newspaper, and *Beer*, our quarterly magazine, informing you about beer and pub news and detailing events and beer festivals around the country.

- Free or reduced entry to over 160 national, regional and local beer festivals.

- Money off many of our publications including the *Good Beer Guide*, the *Good Bottled Beer Guide* and *So You Want to Be a Beer Expert*?

- Access to a members-only section of our website, **www.camra.org.uk**, which gives up-to-the-minute news stories and includes a special offer section with regular features.

- Special discounts with numerous partner organisations and money off real ale in your participating local pubs as part of our Pubs Discount Scheme.

Log onto **www.camra.org.uk/join** for CAMRA membership information.

---

*£24 membership cost stated is only available via Direct Debit, other concessionary rates available.

Please note membership rates stated are correct at the time of printing but are subject to change.

Full details of all membership rates can be found here:
www.camra.org.uk/membershiprates